SAN DIEGO SPECTERS
GHOSTS, POLTERGEISTS, AND PHANTASMIC TALES

Written by

John J. Lamb

SUNBELT PUBLICATIONS
San Diego, California

Sunbelt Publications, Inc.
P.O. Box 191126
San Diego, CA 92159-1126
(619) 258-4911, fax: (619) 258-4916
www.sunbeltbooks.com

"Adventures in the Natural History and Cultural Heritage of the Californias"
A series edited by Lowell Lindsay

11 10 09 08 07   5 4 3 2 1

Library of Congress Cataloging-in-Publication Data

Lamb, John, J., 1955-
    San Diego Specters: ghosts, poltergeists, and phantasmic tales
    / by John J. Lamb.
        p. cm.

    Includes bibliographical references and index.
    ISBN 0-932653-32-4
    1. Ghosts—California--San Diego County. I. Title.

BF1472. U6L36   1999
    133.1'09794'98--dc21
                                            99-33384
                                               CIP

Photo credits: Except where noted, all photos are by John J. Lamb

Cover Photo: Jo Cryder's Photos

For my beloved Joyce

SAN PASQUAL BATTLEFIELD

Contents

RANCHO BUENA VISTA

FOREWORD

Ghosts. The word itself conjures many images from "Casper the Friendly Ghost" to such sayings as "giving up the ghost" and "a ghost of a chance." Ghosts have found their way into our folklore, (The Headless Horseman of *The Knickerbocker Tales*), our music (*Ghost Riders in the Sky* by the Riders of the Purple Sage), and our literature (*Hamlet* by William Shakespeare).

But what is a ghost?

Many ask the question "Do you believe in ghosts?" The answer to that question is far more complex than a simple yes or no. Yes, I believe in a phenomena that people call "the ghost." I believe it because too many people over too many centuries have seen such things. I believe it because this phenomena has been studied for too long by too many learned men to be discounted. I believe, lastly, because I have seen ghosts with my own eyes.

I have investigated hundreds of cases up and down the state of California seeking answers to the true nature of this phenomena. I am still searching. I have found that far more people than one would expect have seen ghosts, far more than the 10% listed in polls. Many are trained observers who never believed in anything like a ghost until the time they came face to face with one.

Such a man is Mr. John J. Lamb. He brings his skill as a police investigator to the quest to solve this, perhaps the greatest of all mysteries. He goes beyond the mere collecting of stories on finds in so many books on the paranormal. He goes out and investigates, asks the hard questions and, yes, uncovers answers. Many of the sites he lists are ones found in other works but he has gone out of his way to document the cases and show them in a new and insightful way. Some events, like the sighting of the phantom dog "Dolly" at the Whaley House, were witnessed by the author himself while giving a tour of San Diego's Old Town.

If there is one trait I admire in Mr. Lamb's work, it is his open minded approach to the subject. There is a healthy skepticism in his investigations. When the evidence isn't there to confirm a phantom he is open enough to say so. When he has enough data to make a compelling case for a haunted location he is brave enough to declare it as truly ghost infested.

It isn't easy being a ghost hunter. Skeptics scoff and see you as nothing more than a scam artist (every fake medium tars all psychic research with this brush), religious right-wingers see you as in a league with Satan (you would be surprised at my hate mail), new age thinkers condemn your research as worthless because they believe they have all the answers (given to them via spirit channeling). Many just dismiss you as another nut basking in the California sunshine—three bricks short of a load. Only those individuals who have seen a ghost themselves come forward to help and offer their own eye witness accounts. It can be said that seeing a ghost is one of the most profound experiences one can behold. It was for me when two decades ago I chanced to encounter a ghostly monk at Mission San Antonio de Padua one night. Though this happened so long ago, it is frozen in my mind as surely as if the sighting occurred yesterday. I believe the same can be said of Mr. Lamb when he saw the wandering shade of a Confederate soldier in Gettysburg.

Mr. Lamb has done the work and put together an important book on the many places rumored to have ghosts in San Diego and surrounding areas. His narration will both mystify and surprise you. You may find yourself using it as a ghostly guide book to some of the most historical and colorful places in southern California. Who knows, maybe you will have your own encounter with the unknown!

Do ghosts exist? I am convinced of it. After reading this book you too may well believe such things are possible.

—Richard Senate, Author
Ghost Stalker's Guide to Haunted California

OLD TOWN PLAZA

PREFACE

Ghosts are as old as the human race. For thousands of years people have reported seeing phantoms and I don't doubt our descendants will perpetuate this uncanny tradition. But just what are ghosts?

Mainstream paranormal researchers usually divide spectral phenomena into two categories: *ghosts* and *psychic imprints*. The revenant is the animate spirit of a deceased human that has somehow become locked to a physical place. This sort of apparition can demonstrate a distinctive personality, intelligence and some awareness of the human observer. Conversely, it is the lack of both personality and interactivity that marks the place memory specter. The ghost's performance never varies. It is always seen in the same locale and engaged in the same behavior, leaving the witness with the sense he or she is watching an unearthly video recording.

Regardless of the type of ghost, all are essentially "seen" in the same manner. One of the best theories to describe this mechanism was offered by G.N.M. Tyrrell, a member of the British Society for Psychical Research, who suggested that apparitions had no genuine visual reality, but were actually telepathic hallucinations generated by the witness's mind. To explain, think of your brain as a pre-cable television set and imagine the ghost as a small television station. Upon entering a haunted place our brain might receive the ethereal broadcast signal and convert it into a phantasmagoric image. Those persons who by chance are tuned to the proper mental frequency will "see" a ghost, while their companions may observe nothing.

The physical phase of a haunting is known as *poltergeist* activity.

Poltergeist means "noisy" or "racketing ghost" in German. The poltergeist is almost never seen and manifests its presence by manipulating the physical environment. Doors are slammed and personal possessions temporarily hidden; toilets are sometimes flushed and disembodied raps erupt from the walls, floors, and ceilings. In rare instances these episodes can be quite destructive, but more often the poltergeist behaves as a harmless and unimaginative practical joker.

One other note: ghosts never say, "Boo!" In fact, they almost never speak, which is a shame because if they could, we might induce the spirits to take a moment from their spooky errands and explain the purpose and mechanism of a haunting. Until that happens however, paranormal researchers can only log the evidence, analyze the data, and conjecture on why ghosts exist.

Readers are entitled to know the credentials of an author before they can reasonably derive any conclusions regarding the validity of his or her work. This is particularly true when the subject is as nebulous as ghost phenomena. The fact is that anyone with a casual interest in spooks can hang up a shingle claiming they are an authority on matters paranormal. For this reason, I'd like to offer some background information.

I first became interested in specters and haunted places in 1994, when I saw the apparition of a Confederate soldier inside a gift shop in Gettysburg, Pennsylvania. Prior to that event, I was a disinterested skeptic regarding ghosts, but the sighting forced me to reassess my views. In the months that followed I read everything available on ghost phenomena in an effort to understand my experience. A few of the books were useful, but the quality of the remainder ran the gamut from innocently foolish to deliberately false.

I realized that I was uniquely suited to conduct my own ghost research, due to my extensive background in criminal investigation, the result of over two decades in law enforcement. My service included work as an evidence technician, homicide investigator, and detective sergeant for the Oceanside Police Department in Southern California. So, I embarked on a career of paranormal investigation and, before a year had passed I was serving as the regional coordinator for the nationwide Ghost Research Society.

Although I believe in the existence of phenomena that we call "ghosts," that does not mean I've checked my common sense at the door. As you will soon discover, I am not at all reluctant to dismiss stories of ghost infestation where no strong evidence of unearthly phenomena can be substantiated. Indeed, the more famous the haunted site, the more likely I am to be suspicious of the stories.

There is one other thing I must make absolutely clear: I don't claim ownership of a conclusive explanation of why people experience ghost phenomena. People have seen spirits since the dawn of humanity but we still don't know why. Therefore, this is a book containing few answers and many questions; I leave it to the reader to develop his or her own solutions to this enigma.

Writing a book is never an individual undertaking. Throughout the research and writing, I benefited immensely from the assistance and camaraderie of many people. Unfortunately, it is impossible to list them all by name, but a few kind people must be acknowledged including Richard Senate, ghost hunter, author and friend; Dr. Hans Holzer, the patriarch of modern ghost research; Dale Kaczmarek, President of the Ghost Research Society; Dennis William Hauck, author of *Haunted Places: The National Directory*; and the late June Reading, curator of the Whaley House. In addition, I want to express my gratitude to Elena Jorman of the Mystical Dragon, Mike Hall of the Hunter Steakhouse, John and Shelly DeWitt, and Clare Schwab of the Rancho Buena Vista. Above all, I'm forever indebted to my wife Joyce, whose keen proofreading eye and loving critiques made this a better work.

Finally, to all the witnesses who took the time to share their experiences, I extend my most profound gratitude.

—John J. Lamb
Oceanside, California
March 1999

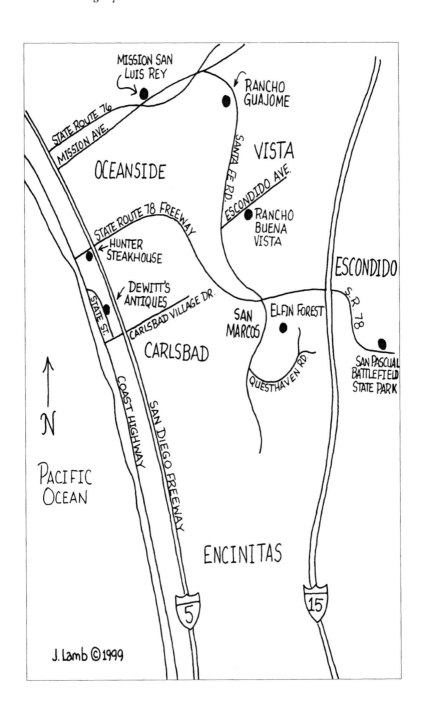

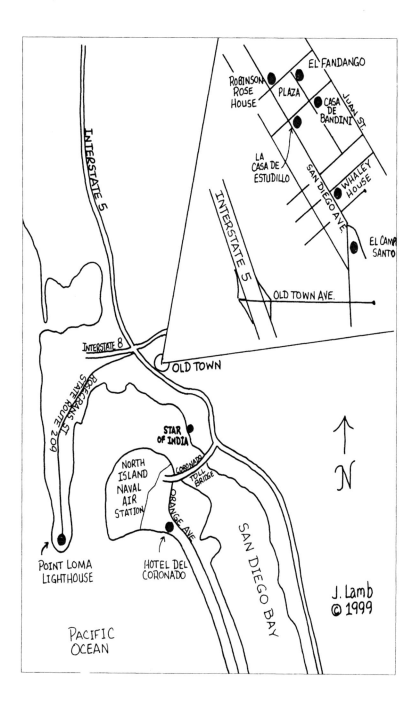

POINT LOMA LIGHTHOUSE —PHOTO BY JO CRYDER

SAN DIEGO SPECTERS
GHOSTS, POLTERGEISTS, AND PHANTASMIC TALES

EL PASEO DE LOS FANTASMAS

San Diego. Ordinarily, the name elicits images of lovely beaches, sailboats on azure seas, or perhaps the world-renowned zoo. Who could guess that California's second-largest city is also home to one of the most concentrated collections of haunted places on the West Coast of the United States? Yet in the Old Town district of San Diego, in an area of about eight square blocks, no less than six locations are considered by ghost enthusiasts to be the abodes of specters, poltergeists and other supernatural phenomena.

Not surprisingly, the Whaley House is the most acclaimed Old Town ghost site. Stories of the Victorian mansion's phantoms have been featured in dozens of books and television programs. Indeed, the Whaley residence enjoys international fame as a haunted house and visitors come from around the world to sample the spirits. Yet not many of these ghost aficionados realize that only a few blocks away are other lesser known, but quite active, haunted places. Sometimes I wonder if the more obscure revenant spirits aren't slightly jealous of the ongoing media attention lavished on Thomas Whaley, Yankee Jim Robinson, and the other celebrated phantoms of the Whaley House. If so, I hope to alleviate some small portion of that spectral resentment.

My investigation into the ghost phenomena of Old Town began with a single day's expedition to the Whaley House. But as new and provocative accounts of hauntings emerged from the other local sites, I began to focus increasing attention on the more obscure specters. From 1997 to 1999, I also owned and operated Old Town Ghost Tours, and was blessed to be in a position to collect fresh witness accounts on a weekly basis. Moreover, on a few occasions it appeared we experienced ghostly events while on the tour. But before we leap into the realm of spirits, I must provide a little history.

The story of Old Town San Diego began over two hundred years ago when Spanish explorers pushed north from Mexico. The Spaniards conquered the New World with the cross and sword; priest and conquistador each played a vital role in the colonization of the Americas. This was also true in Alta California.

In 1769, Franciscan priests established the Mission San Diego de Alcala, the first in a series of church-operated *ranchos* that eventually stretched along the California coast north past San Francisco. Converting the Native American tribes to Catholicism was but one function of the missions and the *padres* pressed the tribes into agricultural labor and tending cattle herds in an effort to make the new Spanish colony self-sufficient. Not too long afterward, the Spanish military constructed a *presidio*, or fort, to safeguard the nascent settlement. The outpost was located on a low coastal hill above the San Diego River.

In time, the *padres* moved the mission inland, in part because they felt the Native American converts would learn the spiritual lessons of Christianity more quickly if they were separated from the rough soldiers. Other settlers soon arrived and built homes on the tidal plain near the *presidio*; first Spaniards and Mexicans, later followed by the ubiquitous Yankee. The city of San Diego was born.

Accounts from early nineteenth century travelers unfailingly mentioned the hospitality of the Spanish colonists, who were referred to as *Californios*. Control of the region passed from Spain to Mexico, but little changed. Life was essentially peaceful until 1846, when war was declared between the United States and Mexico. A small force of U.S. Marines and sailors landed at San Diego and took control of the port.

THE WHALEY HOUSE—PHOTO BY JO CRYDER

Some of the local men enlisted to fight the Yankee invaders while others remained neutral. Many of the inhabitants weren't greatly enamored with Mexican rule, but they were equally wary of the greedy Americans. The situation throughout California was highly unsettled and events began to resemble the convoluted plot of a comic opera.

In the north, the short-lived Bear Flag Republic was declared, while in the south, many Mexican residents actively resisted the *Norte Americanos*. The few battles were tiny, noisy affairs that, on more than one occasion, failed to produce a single fatality. All the while, bickering between ambitious U.S. military officers nearly derailed the campaign of conquest and consolidation. In tiny, isolated San Diego, the atmosphere was periodically tense, but the town remained quiet.

Eventually defeated in the war, Mexico was forced to surrender a vast area of land to the victorious United States; this included the future states of California, New Mexico, and Arizona. Less than three years later, gold was discovered at Sutter's Mill in the Sierra Nevada Mountains, forever changing California. In 1850, the state was admitted to the Union, but life in San Diego didn't change greatly.

In the years before the Civil War, San Diego resembled an archetypal frontier town. There were noisy saloons, the occasional gunfight in the street, and the sporadic fear of Native American attack. In fact, the future metropolis was a filthy, hardscrabble place and considered the most flea-ridden town in the Southwest, a dubious honor mentioned by several contemporary chroniclers.

But by the 1870s however, the original settlement had become a backwater that was almost entirely supplanted by the bustling New Town (the modern downtown district), located a few miles south of Old Town. Then came the disastrous fire of 1872 and many of Old Town's original buildings disappeared in flames. As the years passed, the surviving structures increasingly fell into disrepair. The grand *haciendas*, once the homes of California's original pioneers, were gutted for construction materials and allowed to fall apart. San Diego's heritage was being discarded and nobody seemed to care.

Fortunately, in the late 1950s, a local crusade was mounted to recover some of the city's vanishing history. A few of the ramshackle homes were painstakingly restored while, in other instances, accurate replica buildings were erected on the sites of original edifices. After many years of diligent effort, the antique ambiance of Old Town San Diego was renewed. Today, the neighborhood is home to a collection of fine restaurants, museums, art galleries, and curio shops. In Old Town, tourists from around the world find temporary shelter from the twentieth century as they stroll among the quaint pueblos and clapboard buildings. It is a joyful sanctuary, full of bright colors, good smells, and happy music.

A unique State Historical Park was established to ensure the original settlement would remain protected. Around the central *plaza*, the restored and replica buildings are homes to living history displays provided by enthusiastic and knowledgeable volunteers. On any given day, a visitor might encounter a Franciscan priest, an early California *vaquero*, a lovely *señorita*, or a grimy Yankee mountain man.

The characters lend a sense of timelessness to the park.

But sometimes I wonder if we shouldn't look a little more closely at the costumed workers. Maybe the *padre* isn't as physical as he appears and perhaps the grand Spanish lady just strolled through…a wall. With those eerie notions in mind, let us explore the haunted places of San Diego.

(The most direct route to Old Town San Diego is to take the Interstate 5 freeway to the Old Town Avenue exit. Then follow the signs to the State Park.)

THE ROBINSON-ROSE HOUSE —PHOTO BY JO CRYDER

THE ROBINSON-ROSE HOUSE

Many visitors like to begin their tour of Old Town at the State Park Headquarters, located in the whitewashed Robinson-Rose House. The present structure is a replica of the original house, which was constructed in 1853 and eventually razed near the turn of the century. The two-storied home sat on the north edge of the plaza and was a busy place, serving as a boarding house, general store, and newspaper office. Here a visitor can learn the history of the settlement and view a remarkable diorama model of the original town. Scores of sightseers pass through the Robinson-Rose House each day, yet few realize the building has a ten-year history of being haunted.

Over the past decade, witnesses claim to have encountered the ghost, who appears often as an indistinct misty human form, but is seen just as frequently as a fully corporeal man. Other times, the house echoes with the sturdy thud of boots, as if a man were walking across the second floor. This can be particularly disturbing for witnesses when they know that no one is upstairs. Also, there are reports of the elevator operating under its own power. Indeed, an intangible somebody seems to still consider the Robinson-Rose House home.

Said one anonymous volunteer, who works in the replica building, "Sometimes, in the early morning and late afternoon, when the building is empty, you can hear *him* walking around upstairs." Then, anticipating my next comment, she quickly added, "And please don't tell me that old houses make noises. For starters, this house isn't that old. Besides, I know footsteps when I hear them."

According to most reports, the apparition is that of a man dressed in nineteenth-century clothing. He has been seen throughout the house, but is most frequently spotted in the upstairs conference room. In 1995, a female employee was securing the Robinson-Rose House before leaving for the night. She was the only person in the building and was checking to make sure the upstairs windows were closed and locked. Looking out the window, the woman saw her husband waiting for her in the parking lot. The couple exchanged waves and then the worker continued with her chores.

However, when she left the building and locked the door, she was confronted with a mystery. Her husband wanted to know the identity of the man who had been accompanying her through the building. Puzzled by the question, the worker said she had been alone. But her husband insisted that he had seen a man at the adjoining window, a man wearing an old-fashioned white shirt and long black bow tie. It seemed clear to the husband that this costumed man was assisting the woman with her task. Yet she had been utterly alone in the building.

Others have also seen an apparition matching this same general description. Park employees, volunteers and visitors have occasionally glimpsed the fleeting specter in the conference room, the attic loft, and the downstairs corridor, most frequently in the early morning and late afternoon.

Some park employees and volunteers, however, are skeptical of the accounts. They deny ever having experienced anything strange in the house and attribute such sightings to wishful thinking and over-active imaginations. When asked about the phenomena, one worker was gently scornful. "This place is a reproduction, built in 1990, so it's hard to see how it can be haunted. But I suppose some people just need to believe in ghosts," he said.

However, the worker failed to appreciate that, even if the Robinson-Rose House is a reproduction, it nonetheless stands on the original foundation of the home. Therefore, it is possible that place memories might cling to the location. Such manifestations may not be ghosts, but might be analogous to a kind of ethereal video image that can become visible at certain times or to sensitive people. It might be described as an ongoing live transmission of the History Channel. Or is it just as likely that one of the original occupants of the house resumed residency when the structure was recreated? For it seems as if this ghost is conscious of the living people who work in the building.

Consider what happened to Ruth Ann Herbst. A free-lance writer in her early forties, Ruth Ann volunteers several days a week at the State Park and has worked in all of the old buildings. Animated, direct and articulate, Ruth Ann describes herself as a solid skeptic in matters paranormal. Yet in 1994 an event occurred that she couldn't explain.

"You must understand," Ruth Ann said, "this happened just after I began working in Old Town, so I hadn't heard any of the ghost stories."

While on duty at the Robinson-Rose House, Ruth Ann had to retrieve an item from a first-floor storage closet. When Ruth Ann entered the cubicle, she closed the door behind her and bent over to examine the contents of a box. She was alone, yet something suddenly pulled lightly upward on her ponytail.

"It was a merry little tug, like someone was playing with me and wanted to make their presence known," she explained. "The feeling was almost like having my hair stuck on fly paper."

But there was no fly paper in the room, nor hanging wires that could have snagged her hair. Slightly puzzled, the volunteer casually dismissed the incident and resumed her search of the box. A moment later, her ponytail was again gently pulled. Ruth Ann wasn't frightened by the encounter, but simply mystified.

"I refuse to say it was a ghost," she said, choosing her words carefully. "But at the same time, I can't rationally explain the event. Something definitely pulled on my hair."

It is possible the spirit of the Robinson-Rose House is fascinated by hair, for another employee also had her tresses moved. This was Mayela Cervantes, a maintenance worker at the park. She told me of several early-morning encounters in the first-floor corridor of the house.

THE ROBINSON-ROSE HOUSE

"It's as if someone was right behind me and blowing on my hair," said Mayela. "There's no way it was the wind."

Mayela described other eerie aspects of the Robinson-Rose House. Most often, it's simply a sense of being watched by invisible eyes, but on several occasions, she has seen a misty human-shaped shadow flowing along the wall of the corridor. Other times, the elevator, which was installed to allow wheelchair access to the upper floor, operates by itself.

"The building will be empty," said Mayela, "but then the elevator will suddenly start up. Sometimes it goes up, sometimes down, but there's nobody inside."

Another park worker was frank in her response to the occurrence: "When I'm the only one in the building and that elevator motor kicks in, I clear the hallway. I don't want to see who's on board."

On Saturday, March 7, 1998, the apparition was seen by one of my guests on an evening ghost tour. The time was about 7:30 and as we drew to within ten yards of the Robinson-Rose House a man in our group stopped and peered at a second-floor window. Because the building was closed and dark, I wondered what he was looking at. Later, he quietly informed me that he had observed the indistinct figure of a man in nineteenth-century clothing watching us from the upstairs window. The information made me wonder if the phantom wasn't aware of my nightly ghost expeditions and what his opinion was of them.

The ghost's identity can only be guessed at. The original occupants of the home were James and Sarah Robinson. James died of natural causes in 1857 and Sarah maintained ownership of the house until 1868, when she sold it to Louis Rose. Therefore, it might be easy to tag the specter as James Robinson. But the issue of identity is somewhat complicated by the fact the building also saw extensive service as a boarding house. Regardless of the ghost's name, however, he seems a pleasant enough fellow, even if he does have a fixation with women's hair.

(The Robinson-Rose House is located at the corner of San Diego Avenue and Mason Street in the State Park.)

EL FANDANGO RESTAURANT

THE WHITE LADY OF EL FANDANGO RESTAURANT

Only a few yards to the southeast of the Robinson-Rose House stands El Fandango, a restaurant that serves splendid Mexican fare. Like the Robinson-Rose House, the building is of relatively recent construction. But it was constructed atop the site of the old Machado estate, which the family first occupied in 1838. The Machado clan owned huge tracts of land and was considered one of the preeminent families of early California.

After 1855, the property had a somewhat checkered history. Deeded to American settlers, the house was later leased, in 1857, by Walter Ringgold and Thomas Whaley, who operated a mercantile business in the front portion of the building. The original structure was destroyed by fire in 1858. By 1869, the Columbia Billiard Saloon was in operation on the site. Later, a bakery and residence occupied the spot. However, by the turn of the century, all of the original buildings were gone.

The story of the El Fandango haunting centers around the appearance of a ghostly lady garbed in a flowing white dress. She has been sighted sitting at tables, gliding across the restaurant and passing through walls. Most witnesses claim the phantom's face wears a sad or angry expression. The combination of white apparel and unhappy demeanor is reminiscent of the archetypal *La Llorona*, a female ghost seen throughout Mexico and the American southwest. The grotesque tale of *La Llorona* is essentially the same regardless of where she is seen:

EL FANDANGO RESTAURANT

insane with fury over being jilted by her unfaithful lover, the lady murdered their two children and now wanders eternity wailing and trying to pay penance for the infanticide. But since nary a sob has been heard from El Fandango's specter and no children were murdered on the site, it is unlikely this ghost is San Diego's version of *La Llorona*.

A framed newspaper story commemorates the spot where a diner observed the ghost in 1987. The details of the original story are simple. While dining in the restaurant, a customer saw a woman in a white dress from the nineteenth century. The spectral figure was indistinct and vanished a moment later. More than a little disturbed, the diner mentioned the encounter to the restaurant staff. No one else had seen the woman, but the workers weren't inordinately surprised, for they'd received other reports of the White Lady.

Although some of the restaurant employees scoff at the notion of a ghost, it is common knowledge among other workers that the former business manager observed the White Lady gliding through the building on several occasions. Furthermore, in 1997 a food server reported catching sight of the specter as she disappeared into a wall near the back of the restaurant.

Another witness to the phenomenon was security officer Zephaniah Cearley. His experience occurred one evening, after midnight, in 1995. Cearley was walking past El Fandango when he noted movement inside the closed restaurant. Peering through the darkness, the guard saw the indistinct figure of a woman just inside the French doors on the east edge of the patio. The woman was attired in a long white dress and appeared to be strolling through the building. As a new employee, Cearley was unacquainted with the stories of haunting in Old Town, therefore, his natural presumption was that he was watching a living human being. Still, there was something troubling about the woman. "Her movement was very smooth," remembered Cearley. "I don't think I've ever seen a person walk that smoothly."

When I asked if the verb "glide" might best describe the type of movement he observed, Cearley nodded in agreement. Later, said the security officer, he learned from other guards about the spectral White Lady of El Fandango.

In assessing the accounts of this ghost, I discovered a common denominator. No matter the time of day or location of the sighting, it is clear the White Lady is unaware of her surroundings and observers. This would suggest the wraith is not a ghost in the conventional sense of an "earthbound" soul, but a place memory or energy shell. Metaphysicians and researchers have suggested that human emotional energy can be deposited at a physical location. The intangible residue from a tragic or joyful event might endure for years or even decades after the causative episode. "Ghost" phenomena can occur when a sensitive witness senses this energy pattern and subconsciously converts the data into sounds, odors, or a wraith-like vision of the person who experienced the powerful emotions.

At least one ghost researcher feels he has identified the specter. Richard Senate, a noted Southern California ghost hunter and author, believes the White Lady is a departed member of the Machado clan. I believe his assessment is correct, but the cause of the haunting remains unknown. Yet I heard a sensible suggestion to explain the sorrowful demeanor of the phantom. One evening, as I told the story of the

White Lady, a woman interjected, "Maybe she's just unhappy over having to move from her home."

Sometimes the simplest solutions are the ones we most often overlook.

I recently had dinner at El Fandango. The restaurant was filled with happy diners, the delicious aroma of food, and sweet Mexican music. If indeed the White Lady was an earthbound soul I suddenly understood another possible reason why she might remain locked to the spot. For if ghosts continue to crave the more joyful elements of human existence, the pleasant atmosphere of El Fandango may satisfy that need.

(El Fandango is located at 2734 Calhoun Street, San Diego, CA 92110. Telephone: (619) 298-2860.)

CASA DE BANDINI RESTAURANT

If your desire is to take a meal at a haunted restaurant in Old Town, you are not limited to El Fandango. About thirty yards south of the White Lady's abode is Casa de Bandini, a fine eatery and home to yet another spectral woman and some gentle poltergeist activity. It is also one of the places that occasionally featured curious episodes during my ghost tours.

In 1829 construction began on the large and stately building that was to become the home of Juan Bandini and his family. Born in Peru and a naturalized Mexican citizen, Juan Bandini was among the original settlers of San Diego. In the late 1860s, Albert Seeley purchased the house, added a second floor, and converted the structure into the Cosmopolitan Hotel. Today, the bougainvillea-bedecked home is one of the most popular restaurants in Old Town San Diego.

An older gentleman who claimed to have taken part in the refurbishment of the building that occurred in the early 1970s first alerted me to the existence of ghost phenomena there. The man told me that while the first floor was being converted to a restaurant, he and other workers had experienced some strange events. These included the periodic sound of an invisible growling dog in the central courtyard, the ongoing malfunctioning of lights, and sightings of a misty, translucent woman throughout the building.

Since that original report, I've received additional stories about the building. An Old Town gardener described having seen a misty human form pass into a wall in the southern portion of the restaurant. When he checked the spot, he discovered that a doorway had formerly existed there, but the area was now covered with a wall. Perhaps the doorway still exists in the ghost's shadowy realm. Until the sighting, said the gardener, he had been a solid skeptic, but he could not deny the reality of what he had witnessed.

Other accounts involve the security officers responsible for the building. Several of the guards told me of an incident in 1996 that involved a former employee. It was after midnight and the officer was apparently checking the central courtyard when he saw the misty form of a woman in an antique dress. The wraith apparently paid no attention to the guard as she crossed the enclosed square and vanished into the gloom. The guard quit the next day, declaring he was not being paid enough to interact with ghosts.

Another security officer, employed in the park during the early 1980s, shared his encounter with the wraith:

"It was Christmas evening and the park was closed. But it was my bad luck to have to work the holiday," began the former guard. "I was alone in the Bandini house, checking the upstairs offices, when I saw her gliding along the interior balcony. Before that, I didn't really believe in ghosts, but there she was."

Even with the passage of over fifteen years, the witness had no trouble describing the apparition. "She was gray and almost transparent and wearing a long dress. Also, there wasn't a sound as she moved along that wooden floor. And, you know, looking back at the event, I had the impression the lady didn't even know I was there. It makes me kind of sad to think of someone trapped that way."

Yet another security officer, who chose to remain anonymous, told me of his strange experience in the building. Although he was aware of Casa de Bandini's reputation for being haunted, he was skeptical of the stories. However, he was forced to reassess his opinion in 1996. It was well after midnight, and the

CASA DE BANDINI RESTAURANT

guard had just completed a check of the building's interior. There was nobody inside and the lights were out. But when he locked the door and stepped away from the building, the guard watched in amazement as the lights flashed back on.

"I have no explanation for it," said the young man. "There was nobody in that building, so I know it wasn't a prank. Besides, other officers have seen the lights turn on by themselves."

But, of late, the misbehaving lights don't seem limited to the building and it is possible the phenomenon was connected with my ghost tours. On our excursions through Old Town, I usually gathered my customers beneath a streetlight, just across a narrow lane from the restaurant. On fourteen occasions between July 1997 and December 1998, the lamp switched off while I described the poltergeist activity involving the lights. When this happened, the guests laughed and demanded to know how I managed to turn the light off at such a dramatic moment. However, the giggling abruptly stopped when I admitted I had no explanation for the occurrences.

There may be a mundane reason for the episodes. Light bulbs go bad and automatic switches can misfire, but I would like to believe that I was fortunate enough to have had a genuine poltergeist providing special effects for my ghost tours.

(Casa de Bandini is located at 2754 Calhoun Street, San Diego, CA. Telephone: (619) 297-8211)

LA CASA DE ESTUDILLO

Just across the lane from Casa de Bandini, on the south perimeter of the plaza, is another well-documented haunted site: La Casa de Estudillo, a museum dedicated to illustrating life in colonial California. It is a single-storied adobe home, configured in an open rectangle with an enclosed courtyard and garden. Stand in that compound today, as the fountain gurgles merrily, and you can imagine life in the grand home nearly two centuries ago.

The house is furnished with a combination of finely wrought imported goods and sturdy pioneer furniture. Exquisitely carved wood and leather predominate, a far cry from today's artificial "Southwestern" look. There is also a small and lovely chapel in the Estudillo home; for many years, this was the only Roman Catholic church in Old Town San Diego.

Built in 1827, the adobe was home to Captain Jose Maria Estudillo, commander of the *presidio*, and his son Jose Antonio Estudillo, who served in a variety of governmental posts, including *alcalde*, or mayor, of San Diego. In later years, the home was also known as Ramona's Wedding Place. This christening occurred as a consequence of an 1882 visit by Helen Hunt Jackson, the author of *Ramona*, a powerful literary indictment of the mistreatment of Native Americans. It was at La Casa de Estudillo that Jackson met Father Antonio Ubach, who had a room in the adobe and maintained the small chapel. The priest was a fiery advocate for the Native Americans and his words had a potent impact on the author.

Both the house and Ubach (thinly disguised as the character of Father Gaspara) later became elements in Jackson's successful novel. Some readers apparently didn't realize that the book was fiction and made the long journey to California to see the place where Ramona was wed to Alessandro, her Native American beloved. By the turn of the century the adobe was being crassly marketed as the *Ramona* House and an unscrupulous caretaker began selling off bits of the decaying structure as souvenirs. It wasn't long before the home was in a sorry state.

Fortunately, in 1905 sugar magnate John Spreckels purchased La Casa de Estudillo and in 1910 restored the building to its former elegant appearance. For many years thereafter, the home was operated as Ramona's Wedding Chapel, a place where couples could be married. In 1967, the State of California obtained possession of the house. A second meticulous overhaul was performed and today the old adobe is a superb example of an early California home.

La Casa de Estudillo is also the site of a variety of paranormal occurrences. Over the years, visitors and park staffers have reported seeing four apparitions: a young man in the Blue Room; an indistinct male shape in the *sala*, or living room; a small girl on the west side of the house; and a priest in the chapel. In addition, people have felt cold spots and witnessed mild poltergeist activity. In fact, so haunted is the former Estudillo estate, that were it not for the nearby Whaley House, this old adobe would likely be considered the preeminent ghostly place in Old Town.

Author and paranormal researcher Antoinette May, in her fine book, *Haunted Houses of California*, recounted the experience of three newspaper reporters from the *Riverside Press-Enterprise* during their visit to the Estudillo house in 1988. Although the trio visited the adobe on a warm summer day, they were immediately subjected to an inexplicably cold atmosphere inside the building. Even more disturbing, however, was the intangible but strong sense that they were intruders. While in the *sala*, the photographer heard something strike the tile floor near his feet. Looking down, all three journalists were stunned to see an expensive camera lens lying on the floor. Somehow, the lens had been removed from the bottom of a large photographic carrying case and tossed to the ground.

After leaving the building, the three reporters were in for another eerie surprise as they listened to a tape recording made while in La Casa de Estudillo. On the tape, a stern male's voice said, "get out." Yet none of the reporters had heard this command while they were inside the home. Obviously, someone or something had taken an overt dislike to the investigation.

I first visited the adobe in October 1996 and found myself in conversation with State Park employee Laura-Lee Loredo. Charming and intelligent, the young woman provided an engaging account of the history of the home. However, when I asked her about the haunting, Laura-Lee's enthusiasm instantly vanished.

In a low and earnest voice she replied, "If you had asked me that question two weeks ago, I would have told you I don't believe in ghosts."

After some encouragement, she related her story. Not long after Laura-Lee started working at the State Park she heard stories from other employees about the ghosts of La Casa de Estudillo, but she was inclined to dismiss the accounts as baseless rumors. One day in early October, however, Laura-Lee was forced to reassess her views on the matter.

That morning, she was seated on a bench across from the doorway leading into the chapel. It was still early and there were no visitors in the museum. Looking up from her paperwork, Laura-Lee suddenly realized there was a person inside the chapel. Because the light was dim, it was impossible for her to tell if the figure was that of a man or woman, but Laura-Lee did note it was dressed in a reddish-brown shawl or cloak that covered the head and descended to knee-length on the figure. The shape moved toward the interior doorway leading to the priest's bedroom.

After recovering from her initial astonishment, Laura-Lee

immediately followed the misty intruder. She knew the museum was vacant, but wondered if perhaps a wayward tourist or costumed park worker had somehow slipped into the building without her knowledge. At the same time, she began to suspect the figure wasn't human, for its gliding movement was unlike anything she'd ever seen. Upon entering the chapel, Laura-Lee stopped short, for the apparition had vanished.

"When I found the chapel empty, I thought he'd jumped over the padlocked gate blocking the doorway between the chapel and priest's room," she said. "So I walked up to the gate and looked into the next room. That was when I felt the cold."

Laura-Lee had stepped into a classic cold spot, which is so often noted in accounts of spectral infestation. The phenomenon was all the more curious because the year-round average temperature inside the Estudillo home is 68 degrees Fahrenheit.

"It was like stepping into a meat locker," she declared. "I'd never felt that sort of cold in the house before."

With commendable bravery, Laura-Lee ignored the chill and pushed further into the room, but could find no one. The intruder had vanished. Laura-Lee then thoroughly searched the entire house, yet could not locate the spectral trespasser.

"I still don't know if I believe in ghosts," she said, "but I know what I saw and it wasn't human."

Who was the figure in the cowl? Local tradition suggests that Father Ubach has, over the years, been repeatedly sighted in the vicinity of the chapel. Perhaps those stories are simply folklore, but it seems just as possible that Laura-Lee caught a glimpse of the spectral priest as he strolled through his old home.

In early January 1997 Laura-Lee had a second strange encounter in the house. Again, it was early morning and she was in the process of preparing the empty building for visitors. However, as Laura-Lee entered the chapel, she stopped and watched in amazement, for the low wooden door separating the chapel from the adjoining priest's quarters was moving. When the door snapped shut, she cautiously approached the barrier. Upon examination, she saw that a floor latch on the door had also engaged.

"There was nobody anywhere near that door," stated Laura-Lee. "And it wasn't the wind. The windows were closed and the adobe walls are four feet thick."

Other doors and windows in La Casa de Estudillo have also demonstrated a capability for independent movement. State Park employee Javier Gonzalez told me of the occasion in 1995 when he and another park maintenance man saw the door to the master bedroom moving under its own power.

"We were walking toward the door when it suddenly began to swing open. Not slowly, but like someone was pushing it open," remembered Javier. "But the problem was, we were the only ones in the house. I looked at my friend, to make sure he saw what I was seeing. He did, but we couldn't explain it."

Mayela Cervantes isn't any more frightened of the Estudillo house's active spirits than she is of the ghost with the hair fetish in the Robinson-Rose home. She told me of a time when she and other workers watched a window in the Blue Room (the label derives from the furniture, which is upholstered with blue fabric) suddenly slam shut with an eerie vigor.

"We had left the room and forgotten to shut the window, so we went back to close it. But as we came into the room, the window closed by itself. It was very loud and it wasn't caused by the wind," recalled Mayela.

Then there is the case of State Park Police Officer Dick Miller. A seventeen-year veteran, Miller possesses a street cop's pragmatic view of paranormal phenomena. It was an attitude I both understood and appreciated. Yet Miller had an experience in La Casa de Estudillo which defied normal interpretation.

"It was closing time and I was helping to secure the house," said Miller, his tone matter-of-fact. "I was passing through the storage room when I saw a heavy wooden gate shut. There was nobody anywhere near that gate. A moment later, I noticed the locking hasp had also swung shut under its own power. I can't pretend to have an explanation. I won't say it was a ghost, but something shut and bolted that gate."

In my investigation, I also discovered other forms of minor poltergeist events in the Estudillo house. Andrea Palmer is a former State Park employee. She is an engaging person who, while interested in ghost phenomena, retains a healthy level of skepticism. Andrea had also heard the spectral tales connected with the house, but believed the stories could be explained naturally. Yet she too had a strange encounter in the building.

Again it was early October 1996, and Andrea was standing at a wooden kiosk for visitor check-in that stands at the entrance to the home. On the desk were two framed photographs, which leaned against the wall. The antique pictures feature early views of the house. Only a short distance to the east was the doorway to the chapel; the same portal where Laura-Lee had seen the cloaked apparition.

It was a quiet and uneventful afternoon, but that was about to change. Without warning, one of the pictures suddenly pitched forward and fell face-first onto the desk.

The amazed Andrea had seen the event from start to finish. Shocked and a little frightened, she initially attempted to attribute the episode to the wind. But the breeze inside the courtyard was very gentle and certainly not strong enough to overturn the heavy picture.

"There is no way in the world the picture could have fallen that way naturally," Andrea's voice was calm but intense. "It fell forward and that could only happen if someone had flipped it over."

Andrea shared other anecdotal stories from La Casa de Estudillo. Several workers claimed to have experienced cold spots in the *sala* and Blue Room. Guests and employees have also reported seeing flashes of a yellowish light at various locations throughout the house. A visitor told Andrea of having seen the spectral face of a young man in the mirror of the Blue Room.

Ann Ulm is a school group tour leader who encountered curious events in the Estudillo Blue Room. Said Ann, "There have been times, especially in the afternoon, when I've stood in the chapel and looked through into the Blue Room and seen a misty human shape near the chair. The truth is, I don't really care to be in the

LA CASA DE ESTUDILLO

building at closing...or any other time, for that matter."

Some visitors have seen a more tangible image of this apparition. In October 1997, I spoke with a 10-year-old girl who had toured the house with a school group. She described seeing the upper half of a young man seated in the chair and was amazed that her classmates did not also remark on the strange sight. However, when the girl revealed her observation to her teacher, she was brusquely informed that there was nobody in the room and that she should stop trying to scare her classmates.

"He had no legs and was staring out the window," said the young girl. "My teacher said my eyes were playing tricks on me, but I really did see him."

Former park employee Bonnie Vallas added her bit of information on the haunted Blue Room: "Visitors tell you some amazing things. Several times, people have mentioned the man seated in the chair and asked to know why he wouldn't answer questions about the building."

Like other workers, Bonnie has seen strange things in the Blue Room. Once, it was a glimpse of a shadow flowing along the wall. Another time, she walked through a frigid cold spot. Bonnie remembered the experience with a shudder, "I've never felt anything like it before. My hair just stood on end."

There are other stories. On one occasion, a group of school children touring the adobe asked about a man in *vaquero* attire seated on the sofa in the Dining Room. Bonnie hurried to see if someone had slipped into the locked exhibit area, but the room was vacant. Employees and guests have also reported hearing the muted sound of prayers in the vacant chapel. Another time, a visitor reported a weird observation in the priest's bedroom: the pages of an open missal were being turned by invisible hands.

Still another legend of La Casa de Estudillo is connected with the periodic appearance of the ghost of a young girl. Up until September 1997, I was inclined to dismiss those stories as baseless. Then I received an intriguing report from a young couple who had visited the house with their children earlier in the year.

The couple and another family were touring the house when the three children, ranging in age from 4 to 7 years, moved ahead of their parents to the gate of the nursery. There the children apparently saw a young girl seated in a tiny rocking chair and attempted to engage the silent figure in conversation. Later questioning by the parents revealed a consistent description of the wraith. She was young, wearing a purple and blue dress, and looked unhappy. When the parents approached the doorway they were puzzled. The room was empty, yet the three young witnesses adamantly declared that there had been a girl in the chair, but that she had disappeared.

"I suppose it could have been a practical joke," the mother said in an uneasy tone. "But the kids were absolutely certain they had seen that little girl."

I too was inclined to discount the possibility of a juvenile prank. If the children had indeed decided to enact a hoax, it is remarkable that they were somehow able to select the most obscure ghost connected with the house. No, it seems likely that the witnesses were telling the truth as they knew it.

My most recent witness to the ghostly phenomena was State Park Police Officer Olen Golden. On October 27, 1997, he was locking up the Estudillo estate when he entered the *sala*. It was late afternoon and the building was empty.

Said Officer Golden: "I'd just come through the door when I saw a human figure pass in front of one of the windows. As I turned to see who else was in the room, the shape vanished before I could take a good look. My eyes weren't playing tricks on me. I definitely saw someone moving in that room."

I wasn't going to argue with Officer Golden, for I also had seen an indistinct apparition in the *sala* less than two weeks earlier. It was the afternoon of October 14, and I was walking through the house with Laura-Lee Loredo as she locked the doors and windows. While in the *sala*, I suddenly became aware of a nebulous form in the southwest corner of the room, behind a sofa. The ghost seemed to be a short man, perhaps 5 feet, 5 inches tall, with a receding hairline and wearing an old-fashioned white shirt. Most curious of all was the fact the wraith was looking directly at me. An instant later the image was gone. Who was the ghost? Well, there isn't any solid evidence, but I suspect the spectral gentleman is Jose Antonio Estudillo, continuing to keep an eye on the family estate.

As I investigated the wealth of paranormal reports from Old Town, and La Casa de Estudillo in particular, I discovered an intriguing fact about the place. Nearly all the sites were either equipped with water wells or wells had been present in the past. Several ghost researchers including Arthur Myers and Colin Wilson have noted the significance of natural wells or underground water sources in connection with haunted sites. They theorize that spirit entities may access the electromagnetic energy of the water. This could result in more distinctive and powerful phenomena.

Regardless of the ghostly power source, the splendid home retains the palpable sense of still being occupied and you find yourself half-expecting to see a former resident emerge from one of the doorways. La Casa de Estudillo is a place of gentle magic.

(La Casa de Estudillo is located at 4002 Wallace Avenue in Old Town State Historical Park. There is no admission fee.)

THE WHALEY HOUSE —PHOTO BY JO CRYDER

AMERICA'S MOST FAMOUS HAUNTED PLACE: THE WHALEY HOUSE

Of course, no account of the revenant spirits of Old Town San Diego could be considered complete without a collection of stories from the famous Whaley House. The fact that the building is listed as an "authenticated" haunted house by the U.S. Department of Commerce is intriguing, for I wonder how the federal government determined the genuineness of the haunting and, more importantly, if there is a job opening for inspector of haunted houses.

Lovingly restored and operated by the County of San Diego and a private foundation, Thomas Whaley's home was the first two-storied brick building in southern California. The house sits in the middle of a busy commercial district on San Diego Avenue, just a block south of the State Park. Its structural design is pleasantly unsymmetrical: the southern portion is a two-storied "dog run" house, while the northern half has but a single floor.

There is one gruesome note about the location of the handsome home. It was built over the site of early San Diego's public gallows. The precise number of executions performed here isn't known, but historians believe the victim total was between five and ten. One of the most celebrated Whaley House phantoms, Yankee Jim Robinson, had his neck "stretched" on this spot. Legend suggests that the archway separating the parlor and music room was the original position of the gallows and it is there that people have reported both the sense of constriction around the neck and an inexplicable cold spot.

Thomas Whaley was a highly successful merchant in hardware, mercantile goods, and mining equipment and felt his home should reflect his status. Moreover, Whaley wanted to provide the best residence possible for his beloved wife, Anna Eloise de Lannay Whaley. Constructed between 1856 and 1857, the splendidly appointed house rapidly became the social nexus of San Diego.

In 1856, Thomas Whaley made an addition to their home, connecting a grain storage building to the main house. The new room eventually became the San Diego County courthouse. However, by 1870, Old Town was moribund and there was increasing pressure to move the court to the burgeoning New Town. Complicating the issue was the fact that the County wanted to unilaterally break its lease with Whaley. A man of honor, Whaley presumed the County officials would keep their word. If the lease was to be broken, Whaley expected to be compensated. But the officials could see no sense in paying for a building they no longer needed and threatened to remove the court papers and accoutrements by force if necessary.

Sandbag barricades were erected and a small cannon was installed in front of the Whaley House. Whaley and his neighbors made it abundantly clear that any attempt by the devious New Towners to move the courthouse would be met with armed resistance. For a time Old Town resembled a fortified camp. By 1871, the tense situation seemed to dissolve and Whaley decided it was safe enough to embark on a business trip to San Francisco.

But once Thomas Whaley was gone, a party of armed men raided the house. Holding Anna and their five children at gunpoint, the invaders carried the county documents away to their present home in New Town. Whaley was justifiably infuriated by the gross intrusion and assault on his family, but could never obtain redress (or even an admission that the ugly episode ever occurred) from the County. Over 125 years have passed since the violation of his home, but it appears the spirit of Thomas Whaley is unforgiving.

The haunting of the Whaley House extends back to the 1890s, when the family periodically heard the echo of disembodied footfalls on the second floor. Specific information on the early ghost reports is somewhat scant, but it is known that Sir Arthur Conan Doyle visited the home in the early 1920s. Known primarily as the creator of the immortal fictional detective Sherlock Holmes, Doyle was also an extremely competent investigator of paranormal phenomena and a member of the British Society for Psychical Research. Doyle, it seems, was quite interested in the Whaley House ghosts.

Today, the more common reports of the haunting focus on seven revenant spirits: Thomas Whaley, Anna Whaley, Yankee Jim Robinson, a little girl whose name is given as either Annabelle or Carrie Washburn, a female Native American servant, and a workman seen in the dining room. The final ghost is Dolly, the Whaley's Scottish terrier. Additionally the house is the site of occasional examples of gentle poltergeist activity. One of the most frequent episodes of physical manifestation occurs in the bedrooms. The cleaning personnel routinely fluff the pillows and, on returning a few minutes later, find indentations of an invisible human head.

But sometimes it isn't necessary to see an apparition or evidence of poltergeist pranks to know that a house is haunted. This was something Kim Janovich and her two daughters, Keri and Kristen, discovered when they visited the Whaley House in early July 1996. Kim is an intelligent woman who, while keeping an open mind regarding psychical phenomena, retains a healthy measure of objectivity and discernment.

She had chosen a trip to the Whaley House as a birthday adventure for Kristen, who had just turned 10. It was intended as a ghost hunting expedition and the trio was hopeful they would encounter spooks. At the same time, Kim cautioned her children not to be too disappointed if nothing happened.

But something did happen.

The family arrived at the Whaley House just after lunch. It was a warm day and the neighborhood was crowded with tourists. The first stop was the restored courtroom, on the ground floor, where frontier justice was dispensed. In this room previous witnesses claimed to have seen a spectral court in session. But all was normal on this day. Kim and the girls paused to examine a collection of purported "ghost" photographs on display. Taken at various locations throughout the house, the tourists' snapshots bore odd images. Kim was impressed with the pictures. Most showed vaguely human-shaped areas of diffuse light, while a few were quite chilling. One photograph in particular held Kim's attention. It contained the blurred and disembodied face of a man, apparently only inches from the camera lens.

The family next moved across the hallway and into the antique-furnished music room. As she surveyed the room, Kim noticed something odd. On a small table was an old lamp with long glass crystals dangling from an opaque globe. Two or three of the crystals had begun to swing rhythmically back and forth. Even more strange, thought Kim, was that the remainder of the crystals were completely stationary.

As she watched the glass ornaments continue to sway, she sought for and quickly discarded a series of rational explanations for the phenomenon. Her first thought was that the crystals were being moved by the wind. But this seemed impossible since the ground-floor windows of the Whaley House have been sealed since the 1960s. (This was apparently because the spirit of Thomas Whaley was opening the windows late at night and activating the burglar alarm.) Next, Kim wondered if footfalls on the hardwood floor had somehow set the crystals in motion. But this seemed unlikely, for only a select few pieces of the glass were moving. Furthermore, there was nobody else in the room and Kim and her daughters were standing still.

She pointed to the lamp and both girls also saw the movement. Suddenly, Keri said she could see strange lights in the mirror above the lamp. Kim studied it, but could see nothing. The youngster then grabbed a Polaroid camera from her mother and snapped a picture. When the photograph was developed, all three noticed a pair of eerie milky-colored patches of illumination in the mirror. They seemed to be shaped like eyes.

"We couldn't explain that," remarked Kim. "And believe me, we tried."

The family subsequently went upstairs. While going up the steps, Kim noticed yet another peculiar thing. The air grew distinctly cooler as they reached the second floor. This was quite mystifying, thought Kim, for it was a hot summer day and the house had no air conditioning. It should have been appreciably warmer on the second floor.

While upstairs, the trio visited the room where a notorious rocking chair has been seen to rock back and forth of its own volition. On this occasion, the chair was still, but it wasn't long before Kim noticed the curtains behind the chair were billowing back and forth, an extremely odd occurrence in light of the closed windows. Reacting quickly, Keri snapped a picture of the chair, hoping to capture the movement of the light fabric. A minute later, the photo was developed and the family was treated to a curious sight. The curtains appeared quite still, but there was a faint secondary image on the photograph, that of a series of vertical stripes which overlaid the chair.

Scrutinizing the picture, Kim shivered slightly. The dark stripes reminded her of a long dress. It seemed to her as if the picture revealed the image of someone seated in the rocking chair.

A second photograph was taken of the curtains, this time from the opposite side of the doorway. Once more, the curtains appeared stationary, but the indistinct vertical columns were again visible, but now on the opposite side of the photograph. Another unusual thing was a patch of pale white luminescence near the curtains. The pictures perplexed Kim and her children, since by its design a Polaroid camera cannot produce a double exposure.

Two other photographs, taken by Kim of the girls on the second floor of the Whaley House, also contain curious images. In the first, narrow, triangular extrusions of faint light could be seen emanating from Keri's head and Kristen's right shoulder. In the second picture, just above the girl's heads, was what seemed to be the indistinct outline of a human face. Was one of the Whaley House spirits captured on film?

I had an opportunity to examine the pictures and, although I'm not an expert in photography, found the subtle images intriguing. Perhaps the strongest argument in favor of the ghostly origins of the snapshots is that they are fairly consistent with other strange photographs taken in the Whaley House over the past four decades.

Astounded by both the experience and photographs, Kim said, "It's a little hard to stay a skeptic when these sorts of things happen. But I'm not complaining. We went there looking for a ghost adventure and sure got our money's worth."

In January 1997, I visited the Whaley House to conduct my own investigation into the oft-reported phenomena. Museum director June Reading was welcoming and provided a brief summary of the haunting. June had been the director of the museum since 1959 and during 38 years of service had encountered her fair share of odd experiences. (In fact, June remained at her post until 1998 when she died.)

"The first time I saw the house was in 1954," said June. "It was in pretty poor shape. Still, I was drawn to it like a magnet."

In time, June assumed supervision over the house as it was renovated. During the restoration, the work crew frequently reported hearing ghostly footfalls on the second floor. The building already had a reputation as being haunted and June subsequently learned that Thomas Whaley's daughter, Corinne Lillian, had apparently heard the footfalls many times during her tenancy, which lasted until the 1940s.

By the early 1960s, the work was completed and the house opened to the public. It was also about this time the ground-floor windows began to open of their own accord. Most often this occurred at night when the museum was closed and the windows had been locked. The burglar alarm was repeatedly tripped and police responded to the building. In time, it became necessary to seal the windows.

The famous parapsychologist and author, Professor-Doctor Hans Holzer visited the house in 1966, in the company of renowned seer Sybil Leek and television personality Regis Philbin. Holzer's investigation was the very first comprehensive examination of ghost phenomena undertaken at the Whaley House and the results of this inquiry are recorded in his book *Ghosts of the Golden West*.

During a séance, Sybil seems to have made contact with the revenant spirit of Thomas Whaley. Interrogating the ghost through a medium, Holzer learned that Whaley was apparently responsible for the opening of the windows. Further comments seemed to indicate that the ghost's behavior was in response to the removal of documents from the building, an unmistakable allusion to the 1871 brutal invasion of Whaley's home.

In the end, the séance made one thing clear: Thomas Whaley still considered himself the house's owner.

June had no doubt of Thomas Whaley's ongoing presence, for she and others had seen him. She described one encounter that occurred in the late 1980s: "It was late morning and I was in the central hallway near the bottom of the stairs," she explained. "Looking up, I suddenly saw a man in Victorian clothing standing on the second-floor landing. It was Thomas Whaley."

June based her identification of the specter on old photographs of Thomas Whaley. There was, however, nothing wispy or translucent about the ghost. He looked no different from a living person and June took the opportunity to study the wraith's features. Whaley wore a black frock coat, white shirt, black pantaloons, and a wide-brimmed hat. In fact, the vision was so clear that June noted that the toes of Whaley's boots were upturned, a feature common to footwear of the period. Although there were tourists on the second floor, all had their backs to the ghost and were unaware of its presence.

"I kept waiting for someone to turn around and notice him. But they never did," June said. "It was kind of funny. So many people come to the house looking for a ghost and there he was, standing right behind them."

Hoping to corroborate the event, June quietly called a museum guide to the stairway. The woman also saw the ghost and later described his appearance in a manner identical to June's. A moment later, the apparition was surrounded by a diffuse illumination that reminded June of a blue neon light. Then the ghost's form seemed to collapse upon itself and vanished. June described herself and the guide as speechless for a few seconds; both slightly awed by the experience.

Finally, the guide broke the silence, observing, "Well, *that* guest didn't pay an admission fee to get in here."

"Well, of course not," June replied. "That was Mr. Whaley."

The spirit of Thomas Whaley often manifests in far less dramatic ways, June said. Sometimes it is the distinctive odor of smoke from a Cuban cigar, usually detected in Whaley's study and the parlor. (Although I must confess to a suspicion of the average witness claiming they can truly distinguish the smell of a fine Havana cigar from a 50-cent stogie.)

A little-known element of the Whaley House story is that Thomas and Anna were a devoted and loving couple. "Theirs was an extremely loving relationship. Even after years of marriage, Thomas's letters to Anna reflect an ongoing passionate love. Frankly, I can't imagine them not being together," said June. The bond has endured beyond death for Anna remains with her husband.

Anna is seen far less frequently than her husband. Guests occasionally report observing a portion of a translucent long dress in the music room. Other times, Anna's rocking chair on the second floor is seen moving under its own power. It is believed the phantom mother is rocking her sick infant son, Thomas Whaley Jr. Sadly, the boy died and this may account for other witness accounts of the cradle rocking and the sound of a baby crying.

But in April 1997, there was apparently a sighting of Anna by a group of eleven children and adults. It was early afternoon, and a group of local fourth-grade students, accompanied by a school leader and a parent, were standing in the ground floor corridor of the house when they saw an elderly lady emerge from the dining room and walk silently up the hallway. The woman was dressed in a nineteenth century gown and paid the group no heed as she passed and entered the kitchen.

Naturally presuming the woman was a Whaley House employee attired in historical costume, no one initially gave the encounter much thought. But when the parent mentioned the sighting to another museum employee, she was greeted with a blank stare. There was nobody dressed in nineteenth-century apparel in the house, the witness was informed. Furthermore, it would have been impossible for anyone to enter the kitchen, because entrance to the room was blocked with a thick barrier of transparent plastic. Yet eleven witnesses had watched the phantom go into the room.

Other times, Anna has been seen from outside the house. For at least four decades, local residents and visitors have observed her image in an upstairs window on the south side of the home. Recently, a tourist may have captured the form of Anna on film. The picture is on display at the Whaley House and I was allowed to examine it. It shows the faintly transparent image of a woman dressed in Victorian clothing visible on the window glass against a backdrop of curtains. In all truth, the picture impressed me as a fraud, for it was simply too good.

The scent of perfume and the sound of song most frequently mark Anna's presence. In the music room, June and others have detected the odor of lavender perfume which research has shown was Anna's favorite scent. Other times, witnesses have heard the sound of the piano playing. Yet upon checking the room, they have found it vacant. The tuneful female ghost has also played the organ, which is in the courtroom. June recalled an experience from a few years earlier when she heard the organ playing the tune *Home Again*, a popular song from the Victorian era. The museum director's first thought was that a misbehaving guest was playing the antique organ. Rushing to the room, she discovered it empty.

But the old court chambers may not be entirely vacant, for it is here that yet another ghost may reside. She is the spirit revenant of a young Native American woman who worked as a domestic servant for the Whaley family. The woman's name isn't known, but she lived in a small cubicle in the corner of the former courtroom in the years after the county offices were moved.

Over the past four decades, various sensitive guests have reported seeing or perceiving the Native American woman in the courtroom. Even more compelling is a photograph taken in October 1992 in that chamber. Using extremely high-speed black and white film, a professional photographer produced the image. In the dim lantern light, it is possible to discern the small silhouette of a woman in what seems to be a long dress. The figure stands in the northwest corner of the room, which is thought to have been the location of the servant's tiny quarters. The photographer, said June, was unable to account for the curious image, because the room had been empty when he snapped the picture.

The kitchen is the base of yet another ghost, this one apparently the child of a neighboring family. Her name has been given in other books as Annabelle, but my research with the San Diego Historical Society seems to indicate that her name was actually Carrie Washburn. (The name Annabelle likely emerged from information provided during the 1966 séance.) Regardless of her name, the girl died in a horrible accident sometime in the mid-nineteenth century.

Carrie was running down the naked slope of a hill (which then existed behind the Whaley House) when she struck a clothesline and ruptured her trachea. The child was carried into the Whaley's kitchen and placed on the table, where she died a few minutes later. Over the years, witnesses have seen a young, blonde girl both running in the yard and in the kitchen.

Regarding Carrie, I asked June if she had any thought as to why the young ghost remained connected to the kitchen. Her answer surprised me.

"Oh, the kitchen may have been a very happy place for her," June said. "The neighborhood children visited all the time, hoping for cookies."

Curiously, there is little evidence to prove the existence of the most famous ghost of the Whaley House, who is most often reported to be responsible for the footfalls on the second floor. His name is Yankee Jim Robinson, and with the passage of nearly 150 years, the thief has become a martyred symbol of frontier justice gone mad. This is indeed strange because Yankee Jim was an unalloyed scoundrel.

Legend has it that Yankee Jim came to San Diego from the northern California gold fields in 1851. This element of the story alone should provoke suspicion, for the gold rush was in full swing at that time and it seems extraordinarily odd that he would have voluntarily left the diggings of the Mother Lode for the remote and unpromising town of San Diego. It has even been suggested that the thieving Yankee Jim fled the mining camp two steps ahead of a lynch mob.

In 1852, he was accused of stealing San Diego's only pilot boat, the *Plautus*. In fairness, he later claimed that he was only "borrowing" the boat for a day's excursion. (And Lord knows I never heard *that* line from the auto theft suspects I've arrested over the years.) In any event, a hue and cry was sounded for the apprehension of Yankee Jim. Perhaps in an effort to escape responsibility for his crime, or because he genuinely believed himself innocent, he resisted arrest. During the struggle, he received a savage blow to the head and was injured.

Not long afterward, sick and delirious, Yankee Jim was tried and rapidly found guilty. The judge, who by many accounts was roaring drunk, pronounced sentence: Yankee Jim was to be hung by the neck until he was dead. A few weeks later the sentence was carried out and Yankee Jim was led in a wagon to the gallows.

The execution, however, was botched. The rope was not quite short enough to snap Yankee Jim's neck cleanly and it took some 15 minutes for the strangling man to die. To add one final grotesque note to the proceedings, Yankee Jim's executioner was his own godfather, Sheriff William Crosswaithe.

A century later the ugly story became fodder for ghost hunters seeking to add one more phantom to the growing roster of Whaley House spooks. But there is little evidence to positively identify him as the ghost responsible for the second-floor footfalls. What's more, the executed thief has never actually been seen in the house and his identification springs from psychic impressions and table-tipping sessions. And, if you will recall, several other men were executed on the site.

Indeed, in *Fallout from the Skeleton's Closet*, a marvelous book of offbeat local history by Herbert Lockwood published in 1967, Whaley House staffers attributed the ghostly footsteps to another doomed prisoner. He was Juan Verdugo, a Native American who took part in a tribal uprising, was convicted of murder, and hung on the spot in 1853.

June Reading had never seen Yankee Jim (or Juan Verdugo for that matter), but she invited me to stand directly beneath the archway separating the parlor and music room. As previously mentioned, this is believed to be the original site of the gallows and over the years witnesses standing there have reported experiencing a cold spot and sometimes a sense of constriction around the neck. I accepted the challenge and took up a position beneath the wooden arch.

I can't say that I actually experienced anything beyond the air growing a little cooler and even that could have been my imagination. Nor did I feel an invisible rope around my throat, which was just as well.

In speaking further with June, I confirmed a suspicion. Only a few feet behind the home is a capped water well. There had been wells at the other haunted places in Old Town and this seemed to support the theory that natural water plays some kind of role in the vigor and frequency of a haunting.

My interview with June completed, I embarked on a tour of the Whaley House. The building was empty of guests, with the exception of a female executive from the East Coast visiting San Diego on business. When the woman learned of my ghost investigation, she expressed interest and joined me. We moved through the house as I snapped a series of photographs.

The tour was largely uneventful. However, there was one strange moment as we walked up the stairs. Most accounts of paranormal activity in the Whaley House place a cold spot on the ninth step. Legend has it that this was the precise spot where the New Town raiders held Anna and her children at gunpoint. Yet it was on the twelfth step that I entered into a region of palpable coolness. My impromptu companion also noted the swift change in temperature and commented on it with a visible shiver.

While upstairs I was able to determine that at least one piece of Whaley House ghost lore was actually of mundane origin. Both Kim Janovich and other witnesses have observed the curtains billow despite the windows being shut. I too noticed this phenomenon in the master bedroom. The curtain in question covered the doorway leading to a closet or small storage room. As I entered the corridor near that doorway, I observed the bottom portion of the drapes swaying slightly, as if from a tiny breeze.

For a moment I was transfixed. Was I actually witnessing my first physical manifestation by a ghost?

But then I realized that the longer I remained motionless, the less the fabric swayed. Soon the material was still and I began to suspect that my entry into the room had somehow created the effect. Was the irregular air current caused by my passing weight on the floorboards? I'm no wee lad and it was likely that my 220 pounds had compressed the spaces between the supporting beams. Like a crude bellows, this pressure might have generated tiny gusts of air that escaped through the seams between the floorboards. I resolved to conduct a hasty experiment.

Walking back and forth along the corridor, I soon saw the curtains billowing as much as four inches. Conversely, when I stopped the fabric was soon still. The answer was clear. There may be ghosts aplenty in the Whaley House, but the movement of the curtains was the result of manufactured air currents beneath the floor. But in fairness, the curtains seem to be about the only thing not haunted in the house.

In the weeks and months that followed my initial investigation, I located other witnesses to the supernatural events occurring in Whaley's old home. In early January 1997, Ann Ulm led a group of fourth-grade students on a tour through the Whaley House. When they gathered in the parlor, Ann suddenly smelled the rich and overpowering aroma of cigar smoke. Ann could see no visible smoke, but the strong scent was there all the same. Then, just as quickly, the odor vanished.

"Unless one of the nine-year old kids was puffing on a big cigar, there is no explanation for the smell. I couldn't see any smoke, but it was right there in the room," Ann said.

In July 1997, a young woman told me of her family's intriguing experience at the Whaley House. Earlier that day, the woman, her husband, and children, and another family were touring the home. While upstairs, the woman's 3-year-old daughter began to watch something moving in the master bedroom. The parents followed the child's gaze, but could see nothing. They became a little disturbed when the child asked how the "little doggy" had gotten into the room. The adults were perplexed and tried to tell the girl that it was simply her imagination playing tricks. Yet the young child insisted that she could see a dog. The group moved down the hall to the children's bedroom. Everything seemed normal until the little girl reported that the dog had joined them in the room and seemed to be following the family through the house.

In my conversation with the woman, I found that she had some general information about the Whaley House being haunted, but few specific facts about the ghosts. Therefore, she was surprised to learn that Dolly, the Whaley's Scottish terrier, has been seen there during the past several decades. At the conclusion of our interview I was left with the opinion that, unless the child was a gifted actress, she had indeed seen the spectral dog.

On October 24, 1997, while leading a ghost tour, I was an

unwitting participant to the sighting of an apparition in the side yard of the Whaley House. The time was about 7:45 p.m. and I had just begun my monologue on the Whaley ghosts. My guests, a family of four, were seated on a wall adjoining the building. After a few minutes, I noticed the husband, wife, and one of the children were watching something moving behind me. I turned to look and saw nothing.

It was then that I heard the wife say to her husband, "Oh God, you saw it too?"

The child, a 10-year-old boy, then asked, "Are you talking about that smoky thing moving in the yard?"

By now I was perplexed and asked what they had seen.

The husband replied with a question of his own: "Is there a misting device in that tree? You know, one of those machines that pumps water mist into the air?"

I looked up at the tree and answered that I was aware of no such machine, nor could I see one in the branches. The trio then told me what they'd seen. While I was recounting the story of the invasion of Thomas Whaley's home, the three had seen what they described as a well-defined column of grayish smoke or mist appear about ten feet behind me. All three witnesses were in agreement that the image was about six feet tall and not a random gust of smoke or fog. The form seemed to glide past the tree, heading toward the house, and vanished when I turned around. I found myself accepting the family's account, particularly since the woman seemed troubled by the sighting.

Could it be that Thomas Whaley was checking to insure that I told his story properly?

In the end, I found myself struggling to understand the motivation that keeps Thomas Whaley's spirit in his old home. After all, over 125 years have passed since his house was invaded by the New Town raiders, certainly long enough for him to have recovered from his fury of having his family held at gunpoint. Then I recalled an observation made by June Reading regarding the unforgiving ghost:

Thomas Whaley was sprung from solid English stock. In Britain, as in the United States, common law holds that a man's home is his castle.

I now understood her meaning. Despite an armed invasion, the conversion of the house to a museum, and the passage of more than a century, this lovely Victorian home remains Thomas Whaley's castle.

* * *

In Memoriam: In early 1998 San Diego lost an unsung heroine with the death of June Reading, curator of the Whaley House. June's passing is sorrowful and we will miss her terribly. Yet our sadness is tempered with the knowledge that the smiling and charming lady has moved on to her reward.

(The Whaley House is located at 2482 San Diego Avenue, San Diego, CA 92110. Telephone: (619) 298-2482. The admission fee is $4 for adults; $3 for seniors, age 60 and over; and $2 for children, ages 5-17 years.)

IN THE DOGHOUSE

"The only reason I'm taking this tour is because my girlfriend is interested in this kind of crap," announced the young man in a sardonic voice. "But I think this stuff is laughable. There is no such thing as ghosts and anyone who believes in them needs his head examined."

It isn't often a ghost researcher can luxuriate in the sublime pleasure of watching a doubting Thomas eat a large plate of crow. But on this evening I was privileged to behold just such an unpleasant meal.

The date was November 2, 1997, a Sunday evening, and the skeptic and his date had just purchased tickets for the ghost tour I led along the streets of San Diego. From July 1997 to January 1999, I'd taken people on walking journeys through the Old Town district, acquainting them with the specters. The business allowed me to pursue my two greatest passions – ghosts and history.

The young man and his female companion were students at a local university. By chance, they had discovered my tour while exploring Old Town and the young woman eventually cajoled her unwilling beau into buying tickets. She possessed a general interest in paranormal matters, while he was a bellicose disbeliever.

Throughout the first half of the journey the arrogant critic maintained a barrage of rhetorical questions and thinly veiled insults regarding the sanity of folks who had seen ghosts. His ill-tempered comments were so disruptive I was tempted to refund their money and give the tour up as a bad effort. But I persisted, little suspecting that before the evening was concluded, a ghost would come to my rescue.

Around 8:00 p.m. we arrived in the side yard of the infamous haunted Whaley House. As my guests sat on the low brick wall outside the home, I began recounting the long history of ghostly phenomena on the site. Soon, however, my attention was drawn to the increasingly curious behavior of the insolent skeptic. He had removed his eyeglasses and was peering intently toward a spot near the southeast corner of the house. Then he vigorously rubbed his eyes and cocked his head to look at the spot with his peripheral vision. It was clear he was observing something, but when I looked at the spot I saw nothing out of the ordinary. Finally, I asked the man what he'd seen.

"Nothing," the disbeliever declared in an uncertain voice. "Nothing at all. I'm just getting a headache."

The explanation was feeble and unconvincing, but I let it go, happy the cynic was, for the moment, quiet. Near the end of my talk, I began to tell of the numerous sightings of a spectral dog in the Whaley House and yard. Her name is Dolly and she has been seen repeatedly by Whaley House employees and visitors. In fact, there is far more evidence of Dolly's existence than that of the notorious Yankee Jim Robinson.

Upon hearing this story, the skeptic raised his hand and asked, "So, what breed of dog was she?"

Suddenly suspecting the young man had seen Dolly, I posed him a question in return, "What kind of dog did you see?"

"I'm not saying for a fact I saw a dog," the doubting Thomas unhappily replied. "Maybe it was just my imagination. For argument's sake, let's just say I thought I saw something that looked like a Scottish terrier near those bushes."

Trying to conceal the triumph in my voice, I said, "That was Dolly. People have been seeing her for at least the last three decades."

"You're making that up," protested the young man.

"I'm not," I replied. "You can look up the information in any number of books on the Whaley House. I'll give you a list of the titles so you can check for yourself."

The disbeliever looked at the other customers and asked, "Did anyone else see it?"

No one else had and I suppressed a grin as the young man's date began to giggle. "Maybe it was a real dog," he said hopefully.

I encouraged him to examine the bushes to confirm that I hadn't concealed a genuine terrier there. Together we poked through the foliage but saw nothing. When he returned to his seat, the skeptic was plainly disturbed. In a small voice he described the sighting.

While listening to my commentary on the Whaley House ghosts, he'd observed the diffuse image of a Scottish terrier amble from the house toward the clump of bushes. He was perplexed that he could not focus his direct gaze on the dog, but could clearly see the animal in his peripheral vision. Then, without warning, the dog vanished.

The distressed witness concluded his account with a weak objection: "But there is no such thing as ghosts."

"Well tonight is as good a night as any to start believing in them," I countered. "Face the facts. Either you saw a ghost or you've begun to hallucinate. Would you rather admit to being mentally ill or concede you might have been wrong about ghosts? Besides, how could you have known what Dolly looked like before I described her?"

For the remainder of the tour, the skeptic was silent, seemingly lost in contemplation. Meanwhile, his date wore a smug grin and she periodically nudged the young man in the ribs and murmured, "Woof, woof."

After the tour, I paused for a moment at the Whaley House. The yard was dark and bushes motionless. I squinted into the foliage, hoping to catch a glimpse of the spectral terrier. Suddenly, I envied the doubting Thomas, for despite my belief in ghosts, I'd never been fortunate enough to see Dolly. It was, I reflected, quite unfair. In the end, I whispered, "Good dog," and resumed my journey homeward.

EL CAMPO SANTO CEMETERY

GRAVE OFFENSES: EL CAMPO SANTO CEMETERY

The spook-infested cemetery is an enduring motif of lurid films and fiction. But the cliched setting is based on a fundamental truth, for there seems to be an ethereal law: desecrate a burial ground, and you create a haunting. When buildings and roads are recklessly constructed over a graveyard and consecrated soil is violated, the result can be a fountainhead of annoying and sometimes frightening spectral phenomena. This unpleasant truth has been repeatedly demonstrated at a tiny secluded graveyard in Old Town San Diego.

El Campo Santo Cemetery is located on San Diego Avenue, just two blocks south of the Whaley House. The restored graveyard is almost invisible, situated between two commercial buildings and behind a low adobe wall. It is a tiny enclave, not much larger than a residential lot and within, the stark dirt grounds are dotted with dozens of white wooden crosses and stone monuments bearing the names of many of San Diego's original Hispanic and Anglo settlers. Just inside the front gate is the cemetery's most popular tourist "attraction": a grave marker bearing Yankee Jim Robinson's name and brief biography.

Until July 1998 there was a scattering of white crosses painted on the sidewalk and road outside the cemetery. Few visitors paid the cruciform marks any attention, which is understandable since they looked like parking space markers or underground conduit symbols. Yet these faded crosses signaled the presence of violated graves beneath the pavement.

The Roman Catholic cemetery was established in 1849 and

historical research indicates that 477 bodies were buried there. But as the fortunes of Old Town sagged and the population departed for New Town, the graveyard was no longer maintained. Weeds sprouted and the simple wooden grave markers were destroyed by sun, weather and termites. Before long, it was almost impossible to determine just where all the bodies were. Formal desecration of the graveyard began in 1889, just two short years after the last body was buried, when a horse-drawn streetcar line was constructed through a part of the cemetery.

In 1933 a local historical preservation group came to the rescue, erecting a low wall to protect a small segment of the graveyard. Then, in about 1942, the dirt lane known as San Diego Avenue was finally covered by pavement. As the roadway was extended along the front of El Campo Santo, graves disappeared beneath the smoking asphalt. Later, local bureaucrats offered an "official" story suggesting the road builders hadn't deliberately desecrated the graveyard, but were ignorant of the existence of the bodies; an unlikely theory at best. Furthermore, descendents of the original settlers knew the ugly truth and repeatedly petitioned the city government to acknowledge this gross misdeed. In 1993, the bureaucrats relented and dispatched a ground-piercing radar to the cemetery. The technicians discovered at least 18 graves beneath the street, which were subsequently marked with modest painted crosses.

Even in daylight the small cemetery is gloomy. Graves are irregularly scattered throughout the small yard; many marked with white, wooden crosses. Wrought iron fencing surrounds family plots and dusty artificial flowers garnish the graves. Gnarled trees dot the cemetery, their branches creating a dense green canopy overhead and transmuting the bright sunlight into a murky, emerald incandescence.

It is a perfect setting for a haunting and, for over 50 years, residents and visitors have reported seeing specters moving through the cemetery and gliding along the sidewalk in front of the graveyard. There are ongoing reports of poltergeist activity in the buildings surrounding the cemetery and car alarms shriek with an eerie regularity from vehicles parked over the hidden graves. Could it be the disturbed residents of El Campo Santo are registering their ongoing displeasure over the defilement of their home?

Sometimes the manifestations are subtle, but no less frightening. For instance, in June 1998 I was leading a ghost expedition through El Campo Santo when one of my guests, a cheerful young woman, came to an abrupt halt and then bolted from the cemetery. Concerned and curious, I joined her and her boyfriend on the sidewalk and asked what had happened.

"I was walking along listening to you when the air just went icy. You'll never convince me it was my imagination because it was like walking into a freezer," said the shaken young woman. There was a pause and then she amended the observation. "No, it was like walking into a freezing *someone*. You don't need to tell me another ghost story about this place. I *know* it's haunted."

And my tours had even closer encounters with restless residents of El Campo Santo. One evening in August 1998, as I was concluding my account of the ongoing haunting of the graveyard, I noticed a guest glance to her right and then gasp loudly. She backed quickly into the arms of her husband and quietly announced that she had just seen the apparition of a Hispanic or Native American male in rough nineteenth-century apparel, standing near one of the gated grave enclosures. Even more disturbing, the specter was apparently hovering about a foot above the ground.

Other witnesses have seen this spectral gentleman and one local legend suggests he is Antonio Garra, a Native American chief executed and buried in the cemetery in 1852. His grave is a few yards north of Yankee Jim's and is all but ignored by visitors, which is a shame, for Yankee Jim was basically a rogue and the forgotten Garra was a bold patriot for his people.

Garra's story is brief and tragic. Educated at the Mission San Luis Rey, Garra was the chief of the Cupeno tribe. In 1850, the County of San Diego began to levy taxes on the local Native American tribes. Garra resisted the tax, claiming that he and his people were not allowed to vote. It was the same situation that had led to the American

Revolution and, not surprisingly, Garra felt that the axiom "no taxation without representation" ought to apply to the Native Americans of California. The County refused to back down and the tribe rebelled. For a time the residents of Old Town lived in terror of being attacked by the tribe.

Eventually Garra was captured, tried, and condemned to death by the local authorities. The chief was led to El Campo Santo and placed before an open grave. A few feet away, a civilian firing squad stood ready to dispatch the rebel Native American. In those final moments, however, Garra displayed a courage and nobility that still shines despite the passage of nearly 150 years. There were no hysterical pleas for mercy. Rather, the chief declared, "Gentlemen, I ask your pardon for all my offenses, and expect yours in return."

Moments later, a ragged musket volley sounded and Garra tumbled backward into the grave. But there is one final interesting note about the execution. Thomas Whaley was a member of the firing squad and later wrote that the episode was one of the most unpleasant of his life.

Personally, I don't believe Antonio Garra's spirit lingers in the old cemetery. The Native American leader was a brave man who had already come to terms with his impending death. Indeed, it seems impossible to imagine such a person would embrace the pathetic existence of a ghost. But perhaps the very soil of El Campo Santo remains saturated with the memory of the killing.

Sadly, the desecration of El Campo Santo has not stopped. In July 1998 the road in front of the cemetery received a fresh coat of asphalt and the white painted crosses were obliterated. Since that time there has been an increase in car alarm activations and sightings of apparitions.

On July 17, 1998, a vacationing couple from the San Francisco region was stunned to see a misty, slightly incandescent human figure gliding along the sidewalk in front of the cemetery. They watched in silence as the wraith traveled about fifteen feet and then vanished.

Later, they explored the cemetery and, learning there were

EL CAMPO SANTO CEMETERY

bodies beneath the roadway, the man observed: "Hell, if you parked a car over my grave, I'd haunt the place too!"

Yet another episode occurred on the evening of August 29, 1998. As I addressed a group of novice ghost hunters in the graveyard, a guest saw a woman attired in a nineteenth-century dress gliding silently along the south wall of El Campo Santo. Because the figure looked so real, the witness, a no-nonsense older lady, naturally assumed the figure was a local worker dressed in historical costume, taking a shortcut through the cemetery. But the witness was forced to reassess that judgement when the wraith vanished before her eyes.

As the past few chapters have demonstrated, Old Town San Diego is a neighborhood astride two worlds: that of the mundane and that of the enigmatic universe of ghosts and poltergeists. From the spectral priest of La Casa de Estudillo to the world-renowned wraiths of the Whaley House, phantasmagoric residents wander the landscape, occasionally making their presence known. Still, no ghost safari through Old Town San Diego can be considered complete without a visit to gloomy El Campo Santo. But you might want to pay close attention to where you park your car. After all, you wouldn't want to disturb the former residents.

(El Campo Santo Cemetery is located on the east border of the 2400 block of San Diego Avenue. The very best time to visit the graveyard is on the evening of November 2, the celebration of the Mexican Day of the Dead. Local volunteers give tours of the cemetery, providing some marvelous stories about the original settlers of San Diego.)

Phantoms of a Carlsbad Bordello?

One of the most satisfying things that can happen to a ghost researcher is to discover a haunting that has never been detailed in print. Not only is the discovery personally gratifying, the information gleaned from a fresh haunted site contributes to our knowledge of ghost phenomena. The achievement is further accentuated when investigation reveals obscure historical facts about a community. I recently unearthed information of such a haunting in the city of Carlsbad in northern San Diego County.

Christened for a bathing spa in Bohemia, Carlsbad was a tiny coastal settlement until 1883. In that year, homesteader John Frazier discovered an artesian well less than 200 yards from the beach. The mineral content of the water was analyzed and found to be similar to samples from the Karlsbad in Europe, and before long the town had a new name.

Although never as famous or successful as other American spas, visitors from across the country made the trek to Carlsbad to take the healing waters. The town slowly grew as tourists and settlers discovered the region's wonderful climate, lovely coastal scenery, and agricultural potential. Later, during the early part of the twentieth century, Carlsbad became an overnight haven along the auto caravan route to Mexico.

Today, it is an affluent seaside city with a population in excess of 60,000 people. Within the expanded city boundaries is the community of La Costa, where the annual PGA Tournament of

Champions is played. A few miles distant is Legoland, the Danish toy company's first venture into the American amusement park industry. Along the coastline, thousands of campers live the rustic life in a beautiful state park.

Sadly, much of Carlsbad has changed. Farmland has disappeared beneath a swarm of new homes and sprawling industrial parks. Yet the original downtown district remains pleasantly anachronistic. Known as "the Village," it is a place where pedestrians still stroll the streets at night. It is quiet, clean, and safe.

But the façade of urban normality can be deceptive. For amidst the array of coffeehouses and boutiques is a building with an unlikely bawdy history. The two-storied structure is located in the 2900 block of State Street. Upstairs are offices and apartments, while the bottom floor is currently occupied by DeWitt's Antiques and Collectibles and an adjoining business, Spin Records. However, in the past the structure was the site of a tavern and, quite possibly, a discreet bordello. The building is also the scene of some arresting ghost encounters.

From 1994 through 1996, a shop called the Mystical Dragon utilized one-half of the present DeWitt's Antiques, but when the space was no longer sufficient, the Mystical Dragon moved two doors north on State Street. Months later, DeWitt's annexed the vacant property. But little did the antique shop owners suspect that they were inheriting a ghost from the Mystical Dragon staff.

It would be unfair to call the Mystical Dragon a typical New Age emporium, for the store features a wide selection of metaphysical literature, ethnic music, unique sculpture, and *objets d'art*. The shop also houses a staff of intuitive readers whom provide psychic counseling and offers classes on a variety of occult subjects. Among businesses of this variety, it is somewhat atypical. The atmosphere is light and pleasant, the employees are sensible and there's nary an inverted pentagram or ritual sword to be seen.

Of course, it would be quite natural to view any report of paranormal activity from such a place with a jaundiced eye. The common societal perception is that the staff and clientele of a business like the Mystical Dragon would be prime candidates to see and believe in just about anything, including ghosts and poltergeists. But that isn't necessarily so.

In fact, it is my experience that the majority of New Agers allot scant attention to the field of apparitions, ghosts and haunted places. Perhaps this disregard is a delayed response to some of the gross fabrications and frauds wrought by charlatans among the Spiritualist movement. Or maybe the notion of investigating ghost phenomena was somehow made to appear irredeemably silly by the *Ghostbuster* films of the 1980s. But I believe there is a more basic and visceral reason why New Age adherents have largely ignored the field: ghosts and poltergeists are elements of the occult arena that remain disturbingly unknown and uncontrollable.

Much of the New Age catechism suggests the universe is a benign and happy place where, when death occurs, we all move speedily down the cosmic off-ramp toward "the light." Yet the existence of ghosts would seem to powerfully counter that cheerful theory. Ghosts not only don't move toward the light, some seem altogether content to remain on the earthly plane and a small number seem to enjoy behaving badly. Few New Agers are inclined to expose themselves to a type of phenomena that is not malleable to human will. Therefore, the patron of a psychic bookshop is no more predisposed to see a spook than any other type of person.

Amy Cross has worked at the shop for several years. She is a university graduate and at the time of our interview in 1997 was in the process of earning a master's degree in psychology. Although she says she is intuitive, Amy is no superstitious New Ager. Her speech is precise and her observations acutely objective.

It was in 1994 that Amy first saw an apparition inside the Mystical Dragon. Prior to that day, she and other employees had noted mobile cold spots in the shop and often perceived the uncanny sensation of being watched by invisible eyes. Since there was little she could do about it, Amy elected to ignore the phenomena.

After the shop had closed one evening, Amy emerged from an

office near the back of the store. It was then that she saw the ghost. He stood near a metal support pillar and seemed engaged in a silent conversation with an unseen person. Amy described the gesturing figure as opaque, but clearly discernable. The apparition was that of an older Caucasian man with a moustache. He wore a black frock coat, white shirt with a black ribbon tie, and a dark Homburg-style hat. The phantom was visible for about a minute and then evaporated from sight.

"I looked up and there he was," Amy said. "I tried my best to carefully examine the image, because this was the first time I'd ever seen anything like it in the shop."

She did not feel the apparition was interactive. Rather, she had the sense she was watching an episode from the past. If indeed the man were a ghost, he seemed utterly unaware of his surroundings. Perhaps, said Amy, the spectral conversation had been in progress for nearly a century.

Another person who repeatedly saw the spirit was Jacqueline Valdez. Despite the fact she is an intuitive counselor and metaphysical teacher, Jackie is positively disdainful of the more nonsensical elements of New Age theology. In fact, she is one of the most objective and rational people I've had the pleasure to know.

Jackie had never spoken with Amy regarding the specter, but their descriptions of the man were nearly identical. Yet where Amy saw the face of an older male, Jackie perceived a middle-aged man whose countenance was marred by illness, fatigue, and confusion. Most often, the phantom would glide through the store, peering sorrowfully at customers and staff.

"I had the strong sense that he'd spent many years in the building while alive and didn't have any idea he could leave," said Jackie.

The dead, it seems, are no different from the living. We are the wardens and inmates of self-perpetuated prisons. Everyone carries the releasing key, but few of us ever suspect the fact.

After numerous sightings of the apparition, Jackie concluded that the spirit was both aware of his present surroundings and was puzzled by what he saw. The ghost never made an effort to communicate intelligently. Instead, he seemed content to advertise his presence through occasional appearances and silly practical jokes.

Karlla Martinez has worked at the Mystical Dragon since it opened in 1994 and she too noticed the strange happenings in the shop. "We had cold spots and hot spots," she said. "Even when there weren't any customers, the place was full of energy. You always had the feeling there were invisible people wandering around."

Karlla described random and annoying poltergeist pranks. "Something would disappear almost every week. You'd put a piece of merchandise down, turn your back for a moment, and it would vanish. We would search the place from top to bottom, but never find the stuff. But the next morning, we'd come into the shop and find the missing item in plain sight on the counter. It was like someone was playing with us."

Among the Mystical Dragon's staff, it was commonly rumored the building had once served as a brothel and it was presumed the phantom gentleman was somehow connected with the former business. Karlla felt she obtained some evidence of the truth behind the legend when she spoke with a very elderly man who was visiting the shop. Peering at the displays of occult and spiritual merchandise, his face betrayed amusement.

"He wasn't our typical customer, so I went to see if I could help him," she recalled. "We started talking and he told me that many years ago, the upper-floor of the building was used as a bordello. In fact, he said that he'd once been a customer of the ladies."

Karlla grinned as she continued. "He thought it was so funny there was a metaphysical shop in the same place."

Still another witness to the supernatural phenomena was Christine Star Mountain, an astrologer at the shop. As Christine was quick to explain, she wasn't particularly clairvoyant and retained a healthy level of pragmatism regarding the paranormal. Yet she too saw an apparition, but not the doleful man. Rather, it was a Caucasian woman wandering the shop. The phantom had long brown hair and appeared unkempt.

"Most often I would only catch a glimpse of her in my peripheral vision," said Christine. "But the few times I actually saw her, only the top half of her body was distinct. The bottom portion was misty like a dense fog."

Christine also told me what she knew of the building's history and said it was rumored that a woman had been stabbed to death with a pair of scissors in either the saloon or brothel. If that was the case, conjectured the astrologer, the apparition might well be the revenant spirit of the murder victim. The mystery grew. Were there actually two ghosts in residence?

Or three?

Julie Rieger has been a clerk at the Mystical Dragon for three years. The petite blonde enjoys working at the shop's new location, but found the old site a decidedly eerie place. There was a pervading sense of always being under observation, explained Julie, even when the store was empty. Her visual encounter with a phantom occurred one evening as she was closing the shop.

"I'd locked the door and was going over the books," Julie said. "Then, out of the corner of my eye, I saw a small figure moving near one of the display cases. My first reaction was shock, because I thought someone had left their child in the store."

When she moved closer to take a better look at the shape, it instantly disappeared. The bewildered woman carefully checked the locked store, but could find no one else inside. Yet Julie was certain she had seen the small human form. With the passage of several years, the sales clerk is still convinced the figure was that of a child, but could not provide any further descriptive details. The event happened far too swiftly for her to scrutinize the misty form.

Yet it is possible that Julie actually saw a partial or incomplete apparition. Some ghosts seem incapable of full materialization and, indeed, the phantom seen by Christine might have been of this variety. Therefore, it could be Julie saw only the bottom portion of an adult phantasm.

DeWitt's Antiques and Collectibles

Julie was also the target of the spectral practical joker. One afternoon she put her paycheck on a desk and briefly turned away. A moment later, the check vanished. Julie and the other employees thoroughly searched the shop for the check with no success. It was simply gone. Theft was ruled out, for the check was never cashed. Yet two weeks later, the paycheck was found on the floor in front of the cash register.

"Both the other employees and I had been behind the counter all day and nobody saw anything. But I turned around for a moment and there the check was," she said. "Whoever or whatever had taken the check finally decided to return it."

The initial interviews completed, I realized there was a pivotal question to be addressed regarding the haunting. Had a brothel previously existed in the building, or was this merely a local legend?

I began my research by speaking with several long-time Carlsbad residents. Several confirmed that not only did a bordello operate on the second floor of the building, but that a bar called the Sportsmen's Club occupied the ground-level portion that currently houses Spin Records. One older fellow told me the tavern catered predominantly to a Mexican-American clientele. Another asserted that three rooms above the bar had been maintained for the use of prostitutes and their customers.

There were also unconfirmed stories of vicious bar fights and even a vague rumor of the stabbing death of a woman occurring on the premises. I was immediately reminded of Christine's comments regarding the alleged murder. Other people, however, asserted that the Sportsmen's Club was just a typical neighborhood bar and that the reports of the murder were nonsense.

The anecdotal stories of the brothel were unsatisfactory in that there were no conclusive dates of operation. Some witnesses told me the bordello had operated sometime in the 1920s, while others claimed it was in the 1950s or even as late as the early 1970s. Had the house of prostitution operated for decades, or were the witnesses just vague regarding the dates?

As a long-time cop, I knew that most brothels have the life span of a laboratory rat. The business is extremely transient: working girls come and go; rents are raised; and sooner or later the police shut down the operation. Furthermore, I found it highly unlikely a house of prostitution could operate for several decades without provoking some sort of official attention. As a consequence, I began to suspect the stories of the brothel were an embellishment. Bar patrons may have occasionally employed the second-floor rooms for illicit sex, but I suspected that no formal whorehouse ever existed.

I next began exploring documents and photographs at the Carlsbad City Library. In the *Carlsbad Historical Research Inventory,* I learned that the building in question was constructed shortly before 1925, for that was when the property first appeared on local fire maps. The data on the businesses that had formerly occupied the structure were interesting. Over the years, the building had seen service as a bakery, commercial offices, an auto supply shop, and a tavern and billiards hall.

Still, there was no definitive listing of the time period during which the Sportsmen's Club was open for business, but it seemed increasingly unlikely the bar was operational during the 1920s. The locals also seemed to feel the bar was open during the 1960s and 1970s. Yet this information did not seem to conform to the garb worn by the male apparition. His clothing would have been appropriate for the mid-1920s. I began to wonder if the witnesses had drawn an unwarranted conclusion regarding the barroom origins of the ghost. Perhaps he wasn't a tavern patron at all, but an earlier occupant.

This clothing disparity also made me consider whether our preexisting beliefs influence how an apparition is visually perceived. In effect, did the incorrect information about the saloon's dates of operation influence the physical image of the ghost? Perhaps, if the viewers had known in advance that the tavern had operated later in the century, the ghost's apparel might have appeared more modern.

And what of the female phantom? Was she connected with the male ghost or merely a transient spirit? Collaterally, there was the question of the murder. I needed to know if this was a genuine event or more local legend.

I inquired of the Carlsbad Police Department and veteran homicide detective Richard Castaneda. I'd known Rich for over fifteen years and he was a little amused at the reason underlying my request for information on a possible murder at The Sportsmen's Club. The detective couldn't recall a homicide at the bar any time during the past thirty years, but allowed that a few stabbings had occurred. None, however, were fatal.

Rich also provided some general history on the Sportsmen's Club. It was his belief the tavern had existed on the site from about the 1940s onward. Furthermore, the detective confirmed that various prostitutes had employed the rooms above the bar. But he substantiated something I already suspected: no formal brothel had existed in the building.

Upon receiving this information, I shifted the focus of my investigation to the upper story of the structure. I wondered if the ghosts had made themselves known to the present-day occupants. In early February 1997, I spoke with a man who currently lives in the second-floor apartment. He too was aware of the building's alleged unsavory history and said he'd never experienced anything that could be described as even remotely paranormal.

But at least one previous occupant had had an encounter with the specter. From 1977 to 1978, Janell Cannon lived in a tiny second-floor apartment above the present location of Spin Records. Janell is now a successful author of children's books, but two decades ago she was struggling to make ends meet. With its very low rent, the rundown flat was a temporary refuge.

"Downtown Carlsbad was very different then. It was more rowdy and violent," Janell said. "I lived above the Sportsmen's Club and it seemed as if the police were being called all the time for fights and the occasional stabbing."

Although grateful to have a roof over her head, Janell soon came to dislike the apartment's eerie atmosphere; there was always a

sense of being observed by an unseen presence. Then came the night when Janell was inexplicably jolted from sleep. Looking up, she observed the silhouette of a human figure standing at the foot of the bed. The shape was about six feet tall and although Janell couldn't see any distinguishing features, she had the strong impression of a male presence. Recovering quickly from her shock, Janell also realized the hazy and shadowy form was not corporeal.

Peering at the shape, Janell understood the wraith did not intend any menace. Rather, it was confused and she sensed the spirit had perhaps been some kind of drug addict or alcoholic. More than anything, Janell detected an enormous feeling of melancholy emanating from the shadowy form.

"Finally, I pulled my covers over my head and asked him to leave." She laughed with the memory. "He did and I never saw him again."

At last it was time to pay a formal visit to DeWitt's Antiques and Spin Records, in an effort to learn if the paranormal phenomena was still ongoing.

I began with DeWitt's, where I paused to examine the old fountain pens and then surveyed the small assortment of clay and meerschaum pipes. Across the aisle stood a glass display case containing several deliciously archaic pocket watches. You could spend a delightful week exploring the interior of DeWitt's. It is packed to the rafters with treasures from the past.

When I asked Shelley DeWitt, the shop's owner, if the store was haunted, her response was unequivocal. "There's no doubt in my mind we have a ghost here," she replied.

Shelley's life brings her into daily contact with the past. Not only does she operate the antique shop, she is also a member of the Oceanside Historical Society. Yet she wasn't overly pleased to be contacted by an apparent antique resident. Shelley told me of her first supernatural experience in the building.

"It was a few years ago, when we took possession of the shop," she said. She then pointed to a glass display case. "I was standing

there with some friends and family when I felt someone run his hand up the outside of my thigh. I was shocked and immediately looked down, but saw nothing."

Stunned by the experience, Shelley's hair stood on end. She moved from the spot, but a moment later a second ghostly caress was delivered to her opposite thigh. "It was like nothing I've ever experienced," she said. "I knew there was an invisible male presence with us in the room."

Since that time, the lascivious behavior hasn't been repeated, yet the ghost continues to make his presence known. Sometimes the spectral man rearranges or moves the shop's thick stack of antique reference books. Other manifestations consist of the transportation and concealment of merchandise.

"You'll put something down on the counter and, a second later, it will be gone," Shelley explained. "An hour later, or maybe the next day, you'll find the item in the original spot or in plain sight on the counter."

Her description of the phenomena tallied precisely with reports from the staff of the Mystical Dragon. Nothing was ever broken, but the ghost seemed to enjoy teasing the workers with his annoying vanishing act. Furthermore, Shelley had also felt the cold spot noted by the former occupants. She directed me to an area in the central walkway where I felt only a faint dip in temperature.

"There have been times when I've walked through this spot and just shivered," Shelley said as she rubbed her arms briskly. "But it isn't constant. I think he moves around the shop examining our merchandise."

Although she has never seen an apparition in the shop, she is absolutely certain the phantom is male. And, in spite of his lecherous conduct, she feels no sense of danger from the ghost. Rather, Shelley believes the spirit is confused regarding his incorporeal condition and the present utilization of the building. Furthermore, she thinks the spirit may be drawn to the collection of antiques. Perhaps they remind the ghost of earlier, better times.

The phantom makes his presence manifest in other ways, as I learned. There are three radios in the antique shop, all tuned to the same local station that plays pleasant instrumental music. Yet at least twice a week, one or more of the radios will suddenly switch stations to another featuring boisterous Mexican salsa music. Simultaneously, the volume gets louder.

"He must really like that kind of music, because it's always the same station," Shelley said. She then directed my attention to a stereo receiver on a shelf some eight feet above the floor. "And it isn't anybody human changing the stations. I've been behind the counter, with nobody in the shop, and that radio has switched stations. You need a stepstool to reach that radio."

I recalled what I'd learned of the building's history. If the tavern had catered to Mexican-Americans, this might be exactly the style of music an old customer would have enjoyed.

Shelley told of other curious occurrences in the antique shop. The shop's lights also periodically fall prey to the poltergeist's tampering touch. Sometimes they flicker and unaccountably malfunction. Even more eerie was the occasion when the lights operated despite the fact that all electricity to the business was shut off. Wiring, circuits, and fixtures have been replaced, yet the phenomenon is ongoing.

"We've had different electricians in here," she explained. "They carefully check the entire system and assure us that everything looks fine. But the lights continue to act strangely."

Additionally, the ghost appears to enjoy playing pranks with glass display cases. Shelley and the employees have periodically struggled with locks that inexplicably malfunction. She was quick to clarify that the locks weren't defective, but that there were occasions when they seemed to have minds of their own. "There are times when you'll try to unlock a case and the bolt is frozen," she said. "But try again a moment later and the key turns smoothly."

After speaking with Shelley, I was introduced to shop employee Margaret Beam, who has worked at DeWitt's Antiques for over three years. She too has had abnormal experiences in the store. When she learned of my interest in the resident ghost, Margaret held up a print in an oak frame.

"This morning I found this on the floor directly in front of the main door," recounted Margaret. "It 'fell' from a nail above the doorway. Does this look like it fell eight feet?"

The wooden frame was completely free of dents and scratches. Even more peculiar, the glass was intact. I next examined the metal hook on which the picture was mounted. It was over eight feet above the hard concrete floor. If the picture had fallen from the wall, the utter lack of damage suggested gravity was working oddly indeed at DeWitt's Antiques.

Margaret also confirmed the ghost's proclivity for mischievous and annoying behavior. She too had put items down, only to discover them missing moments later. Another of the phantom's disconcerting stunts is to lock certain employees out of the bathroom.

"We've had the lock checked by a locksmith and were told there was nothing wrong with the mechanism," Margaret said. "But there are times when either Shelley or I try to go into the bathroom and can't get the door to open. But a moment later, someone else will turn the knob and the door opens without a problem."

When the ghost's behavior becomes particularly egregious, Shelley finds it necessary to read the riot act to the invisible lodger. In a stern voice, she tells the ghost to mind his manners and behave as a gentleman.

"We've had our little talks," said Shelley with a grim smile. "And he knocks off the nonsense for a little while."

But the sense of control is illusory, realizes Shelley. The ghost seems to humor her wishes, but there is no guarantee of continuing compliance. Because of this, Shelley isn't entirely comfortable with the phenomena.

"I really don't care to work here by myself at closing time," she said. "Because I don't ever feel like I'm alone. I keep expecting to look up and see *him* standing there."

My interviews at DeWitt's Antiques completed, I moved next

door to Spin Records, a business that caters to the young and fashionably alienated. When I asked if the building was haunted, the proprietor was polite but very firm in his denial of any supernatural phenomena occurring in his shop.

So, is the weary, dapper man in DeWitt's Antiques the spirit revenant of a former customer of a bordello? Although this is a popular theory among some witnesses, historical evidence seems to disprove the notion. Still, the ghost's lecherous behavior toward Shelley seems evidence of an abiding addiction to the more sensual elements of life. Or perhaps the old gentleman is simply lost and thrives upon human attention, even if it is given as a consequence of foolish practical jokes.

And what is the origin of the female specter? One possible answer is that she was the victim of some long-forgotten murder. Yet there is presently no historical documentation to support this conclusion.

One unorthodox possibility is that both wraiths are manifestations of a single entity. I'm not speaking of a ghost, but a poltergeist that occasionally enjoys masquerading as a human shade. Such ethereal creatures seem capable of employing the electromagnetic energy of natural water sources to operate on a physical plane. The presence of the artesian well, less than three blocks away, is strong evidence of underground water in the immediate region.

For my part, however, I hope the pair are human ghosts. Call me an incurable romantic, but it is pleasant to imagine the spectral couple spends their evenings dancing in DeWitt's Antiques to the sweet Mexican tunes.

(*DeWitt's Antiques is located at 2946 State Street, Carlsbad, CA 92008.*)

ELFIN FOREST ESCONDIDO CREEK

SPOOK OR SPOOF?
THE WHITE LADY OF
THE ELFIN FOREST

For at least fifty years she has been rumored to silently glide through the Elfin Forest. She is the White Lady and the most entertaining account of her spectral journeys is told in Gail White's book, *Haunted San Diego*. The ghost is distressingly archetypal; a translucent mother in perpetual search for her two dead children. (The most popular story is that marauding Native Americans killed the tots.) Furthermore, this is a ghost that only seems to operate during hours of darkness and is described as being opaque or milky in color. And what's more, some witnesses have claimed to see the wraith mounted on a white spectral steed.

When I note such an aberration as an equestrian spirit, warning lights go off. Ghosts on horseback are almost always colossal frauds. And after two weeks of investigation, I'm inclined to dismiss the White Lady of the Elfin Forest as a regional folk legend. But it is only proper to give the wraith a fair hearing and, besides, the history surrounding the haunting is interesting in its own right.

Harmony Grove, in the Elfin Forest, is about thirty miles north of downtown San Diego. It is located on the northeastern edge of rugged coastal hills, only a few miles from the ocean. Despite the rapid approach of civilization, the area retains a powerful sense of remoteness. It is a region of curving, narrow roads and isolated homes. The woodlands are typical of Southern California. Pale, shaggy eucalyptus trees predominate on the higher slopes while sparse groves of live oak and sycamore grow along the banks of Escondido Creek. Throughout the year, dense marine fog can shroud the area and the swirling mist has often played a significant role in the ghost reports.

Also hidden in the canyon are two settlements that have served to further the legend of the haunting. The first is the Questhaven Retreat Center, informally known to at least three generations of teenagers as "the monastery." Further east is the Harmony Grove Spiritualist Fellowship, a small village of occultists. Both places are reported as plagued by the White Lady.

The haunting is singular in that the White Lady appears to roam freely across hundreds of acres of semi-wilderness. But by common agreement, the wraith appears most frequently near the banks of Escondido Creek, a torpid stream that winds its way through the hills. There are a few other facts worth noting regarding the apocryphal haunting.

The Harmony Grove Spiritualist Association was established in 1896 and it wasn't long before the local residents began to refer to the region surrounding the village as Spook Canyon. During the 1930s and on through the 1950s, the tidy settlement was extremely popular as people from Southern California visited in order to commune with departed loved ones. The Spiritualist Association's village still operates to this day. Yet I learned that this assemblage of spirit-sensitive psychics has had very few contacts with the famous White Lady. One must naturally wonder why this is.

Another critical detail is that from the 1960s to the present day, the Elfin Forest is a place where teenagers party, drink, and engage in fumbling romance. It is the only accessible tract of woodland in an increasingly urban region. What's more, many of the kids who visit the Elfin Forest do so with the expressed intention of seeing the wraith. And there is another group of people who tarry in the forest: a breed of cunning practical jokers whom I admire, so long as I'm not the target of their deliciously cruel humor.

Today, Bruce "Kass" Kassebaum is a captain with the Oceanside Fire Department. But thirty years ago, he was a high-spirited teenager with a predilection for unusual pranks. Then a student at Carlsbad High School, Kass was well aware of the legend of the White Lady and thought it might provide fodder for an elaborate practical joke.

"My friends and I took a white bed sheet, some baling wire, a tape recorder, and a nine-volt light and headed for the Elfin Forest," said Kass with a chuckle. "Some kids were going up to see the ghost, so we decided to oblige them."

The intended victims of the artificial spook were a group of football players and cheerleaders; people who, in conformity to the caste system of American high schools, scorned the more brainy and less popular kids. When Kass learned the student social elite intended to visit the Elfin Forest one Friday night, he and his friends went to work with a vengeance.

"We began with a wire framework and draped the sheet over the top. Then we installed a dim light in the head portion," explained Kass. "Next, one of the guys recorded the sounds of wind and moaning from a Halloween record."

That evening at dusk the spectral assault team moved into the Elfin Forest and took up positions near the main gate of the Questhaven Center. Cars were carefully hidden and escape routes established. Then came the long wait. It grew darker and mist began to rise from the nearby creek. Finally, Kass saw three sets of headlights come over the hill and start down the canyon.

"When they got close to the gate, they all shut their headlights and engines off," recalled Kass. "We knew it had to be the kids from school. We waited for a few minutes to let them get comfortable and then it was show time."

A silent signal was given and the tape recorder was activated. The sound of moaning filled the air. Then the pale light inside the fake ghost was turned on and one of Kass's friends began to slowly propel the glowing White Lady from a concealed position near the gate. The wraith glided across the road and toward the narrow stream.

"I was watching from the trees, biting my lip trying not to laugh," Kass said, smiling wickedly as he described the scene. "And you know, for as quickly as we put that ghost together, it looked great there in the dark."

Try as they might, Kass and his friends could not stifle their laughter as they watched the next sequence of events. As the White Lady's light went out, the three car engines roared to life. Headlights flashed on and two of the cars sped down the road at a breakneck pace, sending gravel flying. The third vehicle backed speedily up the road and took off in the opposite direction. When the cars were gone, the ghostly conspirators gathered for congratulations and a hearty laugh.

"On Monday, everybody at school was talking about the kids who'd seen the White Lady. They said she was wearing an old-fashioned dress and had long hair. But it was just a sheet, a light, and some silly sound effects," Kass guffawed. "We never said a word about the joke. Those football players probably would have killed us if they knew the nerds had tricked them."

Artificial special effects notwithstanding there are some fascinating and thought-provoking accounts from the Elfin Forest. Karen Bale is a prolific author of historical novels and a life-long resident of northern San Diego County. I've known her for over a decade and hold her sensibility and honesty in high regard. In 1967, Karen was a high school senior and one of many local teenagers who visited the forest in search of the ghost.

"Everyone knew about the White Lady," Karen said. "On weekends, kids would take some beer and go up into the hills, hoping to see her."

One evening, Karen joined a ghost-hunting expedition consisting of several carloads of teenagers. Driving into the hills, they were soon enveloped by the murky forest. Karen remembered that the journey had begun with a carnival atmosphere; the teens were jovial and full of noisy bravado. Yet now they had become quiet and apprehensive. On a brush-covered hilltop, they parked the cars and moved out in pairs, establishing a line of ghost observation posts in the gloom.

"It was dark and there was a light fog in the canyon," she said.

"The other kids scattered and I was standing with a girlfriend. All I could think about was how I would react if I saw the ghost. Would I be terrified and run?"

The minutes slipped by and Karen began to feel a little more composed. After all, the story of the White Lady was so lurid that it had to be nothing more than a legend. Then Karen thought she saw movement in the fog a short distance down the hill. She squinted into the mist, hoping her eyes were playing tricks. Another moment passed and a human shape drifted into view.

"It was the opaque form of a woman wearing a veil and long dress. She looked solid, but you could tell she wasn't physical," said Karen. "She glided through the brush without making a sound and then disappeared into the fog."

Karen's initial reaction to the apparition was interesting. "I wasn't frightened, something I find amazing even to this day. Instead, I felt this tremendous sense of awe."

As the years passed, it would have been easy for Karen to dismiss the encounter as nothing more than the aggregate product of spooky surroundings, beer, and powerful group suggestion. Yet she has never been able to fully deny the reality of the experience.

"Was it a ghost?" Karen asked as she reflected on what she'd seen. "I can't truly say. But I do know it wasn't some kid with a flashlight under a sheet. No, this was the misty figure of a woman who didn't seem to be aware of us."

The account is compelling, but there is a possible natural explanation for what Karen saw on that gloomy hillside. There are herds of deer in the Elfin Forest and some of the animals are quite large. Deer can travel so quietly and with such a gliding motion that hunters sometimes refer to the distinctive movement as "ghosting." Seen under poor illumination and through fog, a large deer might be transformed into the figure of a woman, particularly if the intention of the witness is to see a ghost.

Eleven years later, in 1978, Rich Stuver had his meeting with the White Lady, who appeared to have gained a retinue of two spectral

ELFIN FOREST ENTRY TO QUESTHAVEN CENTER

monks. Rich is a burly man who works as a long-haul truck driver. He was 19 when he and two friends took a drive through the Elfin Forest.

"Man, it still gives me goosebumps when I think about it," said Rich, as he briskly rubbed his arms. "It was a foggy night and we were driving past the monastery gate when we saw them."

"Them" consisted of three stationary figures: two monks with hoods pulled over their heads obscuring their faces and the glowing White Lady. Rich described the spectral woman as luminescent white, wearing a long dress from the nineteenth century. The trio of phantoms stood frozen by the side of the road, only a short distance from the stream. Rich alerted the other vehicle passengers to the eerie sight. They too gaped at the unearthly figures. Shocked by the scene, Rich accelerated quickly down the road and away from the ghosts. Later, he and the others compared notes. They had all seen the same thing.

"The woman had this aura around her. You know, like a faint glow," said Rich. "There was no color to her. She was completely white."

I asked if it could it have been pranksters.

"No way," Rich declared flatly. "If I'd thought it was a practical joke, I'd have stopped the truck and grabbed them. But the woman and those monks scared the hell out of me. They just didn't look human."

With all due respect to Rich, however, the ghostly spectacle sounded so flagrantly theatrical I had difficulty believing this wasn't the work of hoaxers. Tangential proof of this theory can be derived from the presence of the monks. Historical research indicates that there never was a Roman Catholic monastery in the Elfin Forest, nor is there any evidence that any early missionaries met martyrs' fates in the woods. Moreover, there have been many sightings of the White Lady, but Rich's was the first to mention her being accompanied by spectral clerics.

But there is a possible explanation. For over thirty years, Questhaven Retreat has been erroneously referred to as "the monastery" by local teens. Questhaven is an enclave of esoteric Christians and is in no way connected with the Roman Catholic church, a fact few kids would know. Therefore, it would be natural for practical jokers to incorporate phantom monks into their pranks. Another anomalous element to the sighting was the simultaneous appearance of several apparitions. This seldom occurs and unfortunately leads me to believe that the event was yet another Elfin Forest special effects show.

Still, this does not explain the luminescent appearance of the figures. We can only speculate that the hoaxers were equipped with some kind of ultraviolet light or similar lantern.

The other possibility is that Rich and his two friends indeed saw three ghosts.

It was time to take my inquiry into the Elfin Forest. Even in daylight a drive through the region can be disquieting. The area is remote and the roadway often hemmed with gnarled oaks. Along Escondido Creek, the mist hangs in midair, creating the perfect atmosphere for a ghost encounter. Street signs are few and I soon discovered it was remarkably easy to become lost.

Stopping at a tiny grocery store for directions, I fell into conversation with the proprietor. When I asked about the White Lady, the man was dismissive and offered his theory as to the origin of at least a few of the sightings. Along Elfin Forest Road, he said, was a large rock outcropping. During daylight the landmark barely excites notice, but after dark, when vehicle headlights silhouette the hillside, the stones take on the general appearance of a woman in a long dress.

I drove off in search of the boulders. There were plenty to examine, for the region is speckled with thousands of pale stony outcroppings. Several of the formations possessed a generic human shape, but it seemed to me that any person who confused the large rocks for a ghostly woman would have to be either very myopic or laden with spirits of the alcoholic variety.

As a consequence of focusing my attention on the rocks instead of the road, I was soon lost again. Ten minutes later, I pulled to a stop in front of the gates of the Questhaven Retreat, the site of so many ghost encounters. A sign indicated that the facility was dedicated to Christian meditation and spiritual development. I got out of the car and savored the peaceful environment. Somehow, in the bright sunshine, it was difficult to imagine that this place was haunted.

Later, I spoke on the telephone with a cautiously pleasant lady from Questhaven. Learning that my inquiry dealt with the White Lady, the woman sighed mightily. The sightings of the wraith were nonsense and the product of teenage imagination, she declared. Then she told me what could be the true story of how the modern ghost tale was spawned.

For decades, teenagers have made their way into Spook Canyon in search of ugly amusement and, not surprisingly, the kids often confused the retreat center for the Spiritualist village further up the arroyo. With its isolated location, Questhaven eventually became the nighttime destination for unruly kids. There were noisy drinking parties in front of the gates and the teens often prowled among the retreat buildings. In the 1960s, one resident of Questhaven took exception to the nightly idiocy and repeatedly confronted the juveniles.

She was a tall, elderly woman with long white hair. In addition, the woman was apparently both fearless and frightening, for she repeatedly sent squads of miscreants into panicked flight. That brave old woman has long since died, but her sadly distorted memory seems to endure in reports of the White Lady.

But is this indeed the origin of the White Lady? For when I spoke with older local residents, several recalled hearing the Elfin Forest ghost story in the early 1940s. Back then, the specter was uniformly identified as the wife of an original settler, searching the canyon for her dead children. The similarity to the Hispanic folk legend of *La Llorona* is unmistakable.

Two days after my initial sally into the Elfin Forest, I returned to visit the Spiritualist Center. A collection of neat cottages clustered near a small white church, the tiny village was pastoral. Despite my interest in the White Lady, the Spiritualists were welcoming and told me what they knew.

The majority opinion was that there was no White Lady. (Minority opinions were quite varied. The White Lady was described as an angel, an inter-dimensional being, an extra-terrestrial, and a helpful forest spirit.) Because the sightings of the wraith tended to be unsubstantiated, several sensible Spiritualists suggested that the ghost was nothing more than a lurid folktale perpetuated by several generations of teenagers. I was impressed by this assessment, for it came from a class of esoteric people predisposed to believe in ethereal manifestations. I also learned that, as with the besieged residents of Questhaven, nocturnal prowlers frequently plagued the Spiritualist village.

"We wouldn't mind it so much if they would just pick up their beer bottles when they leave," one lady said.

In conclusion, the White Lady of the Elfin Forest could fit into one or several of the following categories:

A. A genuine ghost or spiritual manifestation
B. The misidentification of a distinctive rock outcropping
C. Swirling fog in a spooky setting
D. Defective reporting by discomposed and/or intoxicated teenagers

E. The dim remembrance of the brave old lady from Questhaven Retreat

F. The work of imaginative pranksters

G. Deer seen under poor viewing conditions

H. A local variation of *La Llorona*

If this were a Scottish court of law, the verdict on the White Lady would be, "Not proven."

(The most direct route into the Elfin Forest is to travel south on Rancho Santa Fe Road from California Route 78 and then turn east on Questhaven Road. After that, you're on your own.)

A TALE OF TWO ADOBES

Cave Johnson Couts Sr. was, by most accounts, a hard man. Stern, decisive, and self-reliant, this early American settler of San Diego's North County region embodied the best and worst elements of nineteenth-century pioneer spirit. Couts' reputation is a study in opposites. His proud and prosperous family no doubt viewed the patriarch as a great man and a noble character, while his victims (at least those who lived long enough to consider the matter) likely cursed him as a ruthless tyrant. Interestingly, the spirit revenants of both parties seem to be represented at two of his former properties.

The story begins in 1851, when Couts married local beauty Ysidora Bandini and resigned his commission as an officer of the dragoons in the U.S. Army. Leaving his new family in San Diego, Couts traveled north to his isolated cattle ranch near the Mission San Luis Rey. For a time, the former officer lived in a tiny shack as he labored to develop the land.

But as his wealth increased, Couts constructed what would eventually become the finest home in north San Diego County. Known as Rancho Guajome, the name derives from the local Native American term for "place of the frog." The name was appropriate, for the region was dotted with small ponds and marshlands. Even today, the nighttime atmosphere of Rancho Guajome rings with a discordant symphony by thousands of croaking amphibians.

In time, Couts became a land baron, acquiring the Rancho

Buena Vista, the Rancho Vallecitos de San Marcos, and Rancho La Jolla; in total some 20,000 acres of land spread across much of the present day cities of Oceanside, Vista, and San Marcos. Yet his burgeoning financial success, community standing, and status as a loving husband and father could not conceal some of the more unattractive aspects of Couts' personality. To whit:

In 1855, Couts was twice indicted by the county grand jury; charged with having savagely whipped his Native American laborers with a *reata*, or lariat. He escaped conviction on both counts. In 1863, there was an amazingly unmerciful attack on a funeral party at the nearby Mission San Luis Rey. Couts owned the mission lands and refused to allow Don Alvarado, owner of the adjoining Rancho Santa Margarita to be buried in the cemetery. The reason given was that there was a smallpox epidemic underway and Couts feared the disease would be spread when the gravediggers shifted corpses to make room for Don Alvarado. Ignoring Couts' edict, the funeral party traveled to the cemetery where they were confronted by the land baron, his brother William Couts (who was the local deputy sheriff), and a party of armed *vaqueros*. A few moments later gunfire erupted and one of the mourners was killed and another two wounded. Not surprisingly, Couts was exonerated.

In 1865, Cave and William Couts were again the focus of an investigation, charged with having murdered four Indians and a Negro during a violent campaign to evict squatters from the Rancho Guajome. The charges were later dismissed.

Then, in 1866, Cave was involved in another scrape with the law when he killed a former employee named Juan Mendoza with a double-barreled shotgun. The killing occurred in broad daylight in the central plaza of Old Town San Diego. When authorities inquired into Couts's sixth murder in three years, they learned that the unarmed victim had made some general threats against the wealthy landholder. This was considered sufficient evidence to demonstrate that Couts had acted in self-defense. The powerful rancher was acquitted of the homicide charge.

Can anybody see a pattern here?

Even allowing for the bigoted performance of the legal system in mid-nineteenth century San Diego, (all Couts' victims were minorities), one thing is utterly clear. Cave Johnson Couts was accustomed to having his way and wasn't at all reluctant to employ his power and wealth to secure a favorable result from the local judiciary.

And, as if a reputation for cold-blooded killing weren't enough, Cave Couts was considered the premier sheep rustler in north San Diego County. Local Native Americans frequently complained that Couts' *vaqueros* were decimating their livestock herds. Again, local law enforcement (in the form of brother and Deputy Sheriff William Couts) failed to act on the reports.

On the domestic front, Couts was also busy. He sired ten children and built a cattle and agricultural empire. Although a Protestant until the last years of his life, Couts had constructed a Roman Catholic chapel at the Rancho Guajome and his children were raised in that faith. As one of the foremost scions of the "Anglo-Hispanic" aristocracy, Couts was often host to the wealthy and famous, among them author Helen Hunt Jackson and General Ulysses S. Grant.

Regarding the latter visitor, there is a humorous and unsubstantiated story that clearly illustrates an aspect of Ysidora Bandini Couts' personality. She was no shrinking violet and had developed a reputation as a humorless martinet. After the Civil War, General Grant visited the house and Ysidora was allegedly so disgusted by his drinking and uncouth manners that she brusquely told the Union Army hero to leave her house immediately. It seems both Ysidora and Cave had some fairly clear views on both proper etiquette and their social station.

In 1874, Couts was felled by an aneurysm and died in San Diego. He was only 53 years old. In time, the family lands were sold off, parcel by parcel, until little property remained. Meanwhile, the fabled Rancho Guajome quickly began to deteriorate. By the 1960s, the adobe homestead was in ruins and all but forgotten.

Yet in 1972, the house was rescued by a local cooperative of historical preservationists, which was later joined in the effort by the County of San Diego. The work was painstaking and slow, for the restoration team wanted to accurately recreate the rustic splendor of the sprawling hacienda. And, as the house was refurbished, stories began to circulate that it was haunted. Learning of those accounts in 1997, I decided to investigate.

Today, the Rancho Guajome is part of the much larger Guajome Regional Park, administered by the San Diego County park system. The adobe lies in a verdant depression, surrounded by brush and cacti-covered hills. To the east is North Santa Fe Road, built on the path of the original *Camino Nacional.* Approximately three miles to the west is the Mission San Luis Rey. Although suburbia is slowly advancing toward the adobe, the region retains a pastoral flavor. Wildcats, raccoons, and possums call the vale home and the red-tailed hawk is still the monarch of the local skies. At night, coyotes sing their mournful tunes to the moon.

Getting out of my car at the rancho, I peered in astonishment at the complex of buildings. When this region was still wilderness, the Rancho Guajome must have been a spectacular place. Constructed from both adobe bricks and wood, the stark white hacienda is a large open rectangle of interconnected rooms. There is a fountain in the paved central courtyard and mounted atop the west entrance to the compound is a diminutive belfry. Adjoining the hacienda is a large restored chapel and, to the east of the home, are the stables. Wander the grounds and one thing becomes abundantly clear: this was the home of a wealthy and powerful family.

Dan Smith and his wife Joaei are resident caretakers at the Rancho Guajome. I met Dan one afternoon in early April 1997. The spring weather was freakish. To the southeast, an enormous bank of thunderheads was slowly advancing toward the coast, while it was snowing in the mountains. Gusts of chill wind swirled through the adobe as we chatted.

Upon learning of my interest in the haunting, the tanned and mustachioed caretaker casually declared, "Well, we have some ghosts here, I think. Nothing to be scared of, though."

Although he has never personally encountered the wraiths, Dan told of some events that befell a surveying team. It was back in 1992, and the workers were alone in the building.

"The crew was here taking measurements of the doors and windows when all of a sudden, they came running up to me and demanded to know if the place was haunted," Dan said. "I told them it was possible there was a ghost or two on the premises and asked why they were concerned."

The surveyors told him that they'd repeatedly heard the loud and distinctive sound of footfalls in an empty room. Knowing they were alone on the site, the workers were both puzzled and a little apprehensive. When they checked the room, it was vacant. A little spooked, the team decided to move to the opposite side of the building. But after a few moments, they could hear the disembodied footfalls moving through the house toward the crew's new location.

"When I told them the place was haunted, they grabbed their gear and took off. Never came back, as a matter of fact," Dan laughed. "Man, those guys didn't want to deal with a ghost."

Dan's wife, Joaei, has also heard the footsteps in the vacant house, but didn't give the unearthly sounds much consideration. It wasn't that she didn't believe in ghosts, but there seemed little point in worrying over something so thoroughly harmless. However, Joaei later experienced an auditory event that left her wondering just how many specters still considered the Rancho Guajome home. The incident occurred one morning in 1990 as she walked along the dirt road between the hacienda and chapel.

"Suddenly I heard the voice of a child very near me," said Joaei. "It was a happy sound. Not quite laughing or giggling, but it was the noise a kid might make if it was playing."

Joaei scanned the area for visitors, but she was quite alone in the compound. Later, she discovered that two children were apparently buried only a few yards from where she heard the sound. Further investigation revealed that one of the graves might belong to a daughter of Cave and Ysidora Couts, while the other is thought to possibly be the child of a domestic servant.

I walked with Dan to the location of Joaei's encounter. It was only a few yards from the chapel, a natural place to bury family members, I surmised. An enormous, spiny aloe vera bush marked the spot. Then I noticed another intriguing landmark. Only a few yards to the west of the graves was a water well. I'd located another groundwater-haunting nexus.

My next witness was John DeWitt, the supervising ranger at Guajome Regional Park, where he has worked since 1978. During that time he visited the hacienda on an almost daily basis, for the house is one of his primary responsibilities. Although John has never seen a ghost at the Rancho Guajome, he refuses to dismiss reports that the adobe is haunted.

"The fact is, I don't much care to be inside the house after dark. Maybe it's just me, but I sometimes find the atmosphere strange. There's always the sense you're being watched," John said. "Then there are the cold spots that seem to move around the building. Even in the dead of summer, there are times when I've walked through the adobe and suddenly stepped into a cold spot. It's real unpleasant."

John then shared some additional ghostly information about the house. Over recent years, two psychics visited the Rancho Guajome on separate occasions. Both later volunteered essentially the same observations. There were, said the seers, as many as four spirits occupying the house and grounds. Furthermore, the majority of the ghostly lodgers were described as being angry or hostile.

"It wasn't difficult to believe," said John. "Cave Couts never lacked enemies."

In assessing the paranormal phenomena occurring at the Rancho Guajome, I'm inclined to categorize the majority of events as passive place memories. The sounds of footfalls and the laugh of an invisible child are both suggestive of a sort of ethereal audio recording that is occasionally heard by sensitive people. But what of the reports from visiting psychics of the presence of ethereal entities that harbor a simmering resentment for the house? It would be altogether natural to assume they are the lingering and unhappy revenant spirits of enslaved Native Americans and murder victims. Specific names may never be known; Couts hurt many, many people.

Perhaps Shakespeare was correct when, in *Julius Caesar*, he observed, "The evil that men do lives after them, the good is oft interred with their bones."

*   *   *

A few miles south of the Rancho Guajome is the city of Vista. Once a rustic agricultural center, Vista has followed the cement path of most Southern California cities. A freeway, strip malls, and industrial parks have replaced most of the avocado and citrus groves. The former farm town's population is now over 50,000 people and still growing.

Yet inside the walls of the Rancho Buena Vista, visitors can find sanctuary amidst the cacophonous urban environment. The house stands hidden behind a canopy of orange trees and dense shrubbery, and recalls a far more pastoral and genial era. A walk down the brick driveway is a journey back in time. In the garden, a fountain gurgles while the tall cypress murmurs in the wind.

The restored hacienda is that most rare of establishments: a museum that still feels like a home. In fact, the sense of tranquil domesticity is so strong you can find yourself anticipating an encounter with one of the long-departed residents. And, at the Rancho Buena Vista, you sometimes do.

The ghost's identity is known. Her name is Ysidora Couts Fuller, but the museum staff lovingly refers to her as Dora. Daughter of the powerful Cave Johnson Couts Sr., she lived in the hacienda from 1889 until 1912. For the past thirty years, local legend held that Dora haunted the Rancho Buena Vista, but I am always skeptical of ghosts whose reputations subsist entirely as regional folklore. As a consequence, I decided to visit the home to investigate. By the time I was finished, I concluded ghostly Dora does not "haunt" the Rancho Buena Vista, for she refuses to engage in the juvenile behavior of other revenant spirits. Rather, she is the silent protectress of the Rancho Buena Vista.

The adobe museum's curator is Clare Schwab, a perpetually smiling woman with curly white hair. When she learned the purpose of my visit, she cheerfully asked, "So, you've come to learn about our Dora? How wonderful."

Was Dora real?

"Of course," replied Clare. "Although I've never seen her, I have felt her on several occasions."

(Later, as Clare described her experiences in the home, I

discovered she hadn't used the term "felt" in an allegorical sense. She meant precisely what she said; she had been in physical contact with the specter.)

Clare began her account by providing some of the building's history. In 1845, the region was wild and largely uninhabited. Felipe Subria, a Christian Indian, was the original land grant owner and he constructed a small home on the site. But by 1866 Cave Couts had added the Rancho Buena Vista to his burgeoning empire and a larger house was built.

For a time, Couts' eldest daughter, Maria Antonia, and her husband lived in the hacienda. When they moved, Maria's younger sister, Ysidora, and her husband, Circuit Court Judge George Fuller, took up residence. Ysidora dearly loved the Rancho Buena Vista, but in 1912 she lost the property to a bank foreclosure. It was said that Ysidora never recovered from the loss.

Ysidora died in 1952. Yet as time passed, there came reports from the rancho that the lady's placid spirit was seen strolling in the garden and through the house. It would be easy to dismiss such accounts as the product of imagination run wild in a romantic old home, but the stories continue to this day. Clare Schwab told me of one such visual encounter.

A few years ago, a reporter from a local newspaper visited the Rancho, collecting information for an article on the history of Vista. As the man stepped into the *sala* he suddenly saw what he initially believed was a living woman. The seemingly corporeal lady was attired in late nineteenth-century clothing and was seated at a small desk, writing a letter. The woman appeared unaware of the journalist's presence.

The reporter's natural assumption was that the woman was a museum docent dressed in historical costume. But when she abruptly vanished before his eyes, he realized he'd seen a ghost. For an instant, the journalist gaped at the empty chair and then ran to tell the curator of what he'd just seen. Clare calmed the startled reporter and assured him that there was no need to be frightened. After all, Dora was a peaceful spirit.

Clare then told me of her occasional encounters with the lady.

Most often, the curator has felt the brush of invisible fabric against her body as she moves through the old hacienda. There is never any sound, but the sensation is precisely as if a long skirt has made momentary contact with Clare's lower body. Another time, in the workroom, Clare went to retrieve an item from the huge wooden loom. As the curator leaned across the loom's broad bench, she was momentarily stunned. Although nobody was visible, Clare felt a human seated before the loom.

"It was Dora," Clare said with a smile. "She was probably admiring the blanket our local club was weaving."

Clare's encounter with the spirit in the workroom notwithstanding, it seems that Dora's favorite place is the *sala*, as docent Debbie Murray discovered in early February 1997. A university student intent on pursuing a career in teaching, Debbie loves the peaceful old house and the opportunity to provide school children with a little local history. The young docent had heard the stories of the haunting, but reserved judgment on the matter. Then she had an invisible meeting with the wraith.

"One afternoon, my daughter and I were in the *sala*," Debbie said. "It was a cloudy day and there were no visitors. The glass door was standing open when it suddenly slammed shut. Now we were alone in the building, and it certainly wasn't the wind, because there wasn't a breeze. It was then I realized that we weren't alone in the room. It was as if an invisible person had come into the *sala*."

Yet Debbie wasn't overly concerned by the noisy experience. "It if was Dora, maybe she closed the door because she thought it was going to rain," she explained.

There is also the possibility that a second wraith watches over the Rancho Buena Vista and this may be the spirit revenant of the original landowner, Felipe Subria. Clare has received numerous unsolicited comments from visiting psychics who report the presence of a Native American spirit in the courtyard. Like Dora, this male ghost is content and protective of his surroundings. Both seem to have assumed the roles of spectral guardians.

With the completion of the interviews, I was afforded the opportunity to wander the exquisite old hacienda. Not unexpectedly, I located a capped water well on the west side of the grounds, only a few yards from the house. Later, I paused to inspect the lovely garden and my thoughts turned to Ysidora Couts Fuller. If the stories of the haunting were true, Dora was a singular ghost. She was happy with her home and pleased to share it with others.

It's an example from which we all might profit.

*　　　　*　　　　*

Only one question remains; has the specter of Cave Johnson Couts Sr. ever been encountered at either of the haciendas? Does he wander the hallways of his old homes, seeking forgiveness for his lawless and lethal behavior? The answer is no. Couts rests, in apparent peace, at Mount Calvary Cemetery in San Diego.

Sometimes there just isn't any justice.

(The Rancho Guajome is located at 2210 North Santa Fe Road, Oceanside, CA 92056. The Rancho Buena Vista is located at 640 Alta Vista Drive, Vista, CA 92083.)

A Trio of
Equivocal
San Diego Haunts

Although I do believe in ghosts, this does not translate to a complete abandonment of critical thinking. The country is chock-full of famous haunts, but the reputations of many such places subsist almost entirely on folklore or psychic impressions, which can frequently be found to be at odds with known historical facts. Indeed, the ghost might be real, but the story offered to show the origin of the haunting could be pure humbug.

Which brings us to the purpose of this chapter. A variety of ghost books have listed several San Diego County places as haunted. Since I lived but ten minutes from the closest site and a mere forty minutes from the furthest, I resolved to conduct my own inquiries into the alleged supernatural phenomena. In some instances, what I learned wasn't particularly conducive to furthering the proposition that some of the hauntings are genuine. I also obtained some strange reports that defy explanation.

However, if ghost research is to have any genuine purpose beyond idle entertainment, the full story must be told.

*　　　*　　　*

The Mission San Luis Rey, in Oceanside, is listed in Dennis William Hauck's fine and amazingly inclusive work, *Haunted Places: The National Directory*. Yet I found the assertion fairly astounding, for I'd worked as a cop in that city since 1982 and could not recall even a whisper of paranormal events occurring at the "King of the Missions."

MISSION SAN LUIS REY

Named for the canonized French monarch, Louis IX, the mission was founded in 1789 by the ubiquitous Franciscans. The complex sits on a low flat hill, a short distance from a narrow river of the same name. Not merely a religious outpost, the mission was also a huge rancho. Tens of thousands of cattle grazed on the surrounding hills while the river's floodplain was farmed.

In common with other missions, the local Native Americans of the *Luiseno* tribe were instructed in the Roman Catholic faith and put to work throughout the rancho. Often the life of a mission Indian was little different from outright slavery. However, contemporary chroniclers considered the Native Americans of the Mission San Luis Rey relatively well treated. The *Luisenos* weren't consulted for their opinion on the matter.

When the Mexican government secularized the missions, the Franciscans were evicted. In 1846, American troops led by Kit Carson and General Stephen Kearney, briefly stayed at the mission. The following year, the Mormon Battalion arrived after a remarkable overland march from Iowa and took up temporary residence at San

Luis Rey. By this time, weather, abandonment, and outright vandalism had wrought havoc. The church buildings were in poor shape.

In 1865, in one of the final executive orders by President Abraham Lincoln, the missions were formally returned to the Catholic Church. But at San Luis Rey, restoration work didn't begin until 1892. It took many years of diligent labor to renovate the crumbling adobe. The other California missions are uniformly lovely, but few evoke San Luis Rey's sense of sheer power. Indeed, the building is a splendid ecclesiastical fort. These days, the mission is a parish church surrounded by homes, apartments, and strip malls. The churchyard is an oasis of lush vegetation and placid spirituality amidst the ugly urban sprawl.

Yet visiting the mission on a weekday, during the school year, can be hazardous to the ears. Nearly two hundred boisterous, shouting fourth-grade kids were on the grounds. The comment of one young lad remained with me. While surveying the superb and gaudy explosion of colors, statuary, and candles within the shrine to the Virgin Mary, the boy loudly announced, "Dude, it's like a Dennis Rodman church!"

Near the entrance to the small mission museum, I spoke with a volunteer docent regarding the possibility that the church grounds were haunted. The older gentleman had no personal encounters with the ghosts, but did recall a story from the 1980s. There were rumors that an unidentified person had observed the specter of a priest one evening. The episode allegedly occurred in an upstairs corridor of the retreat center, which lies to the west of the mission church. However, the museum volunteer was quick to add that nobody else had reported anything supernatural in years and he was inclined to reject the story.

The next two employees contacted claimed to know nothing of the reports of haunting and both seemed somewhat amused that a grown man was searching for ghosts. Then I spoke with a lady in the mission administration office. When I inquired if there were any truth to the rumors of a specter seen in the retreat center, the woman's lip curled unpleasantly. I was courteously but curtly informed there were no such things as ghosts and that the mission was definitely not haunted. The woman then returned to her work; it was abundantly clear I had been dismissed.

I next spoke with older residents of the neighborhood. One man recalled that some small portions of the old Walt Disney television program *Zorro* were filmed at the mission in the late 1950s. In several of the episodes, a fake phantom priest (Zorro in a secondary disguise) played a pivotal role in the story. My witness wondered if the popular TV show hadn't given birth to the stories of the spectral padre.

At this point my research became quite arduous since it involved watching *Zorro* on the Disney Channel. Fortuitously, I was soon able to confirm that exterior sequences of the program had been filmed at the Mission San Luis Rey. Furthermore, there was a plot line involving a ghostly priest called the "Mad Monk." Could this have spawned the haunting?

Further muddying the issue of the unearthly cleric is the fact that other California missions are allegedly home to similar phenomenon. The sites include San Juan Capistrano, Mission San Fernando, and Mission La Purisima. All boast some form of ghostly priest. As a consequence, I am inclined to believe that the ghost of the Mission San Luis Rey is likely a bit of generic Golden State folklore. And even if there is a specter, nobody at the mission is likely to admit it.

(The Mission San Luis Rey is located at 4040 Mission Avenue, Oceanside, CA 92057.)

*　　　　　*　　　　　*

The Point Loma Lighthouse is a picturesque testament to poor planning. Constructed over 400 feet above the entrance to San Diego Bay, the lighthouse was soon discovered to be at too great an elevation to be of much use to ships entering the harbor. Furthermore, the warning beacon was often invisible behind a gray wall of low marine cloud. Built in 1855 and abandoned a few decades later, the restored lighthouse is now a part of the Cabrillo National Monument and operated by the U.S. National Park Service.

The structure is located on the southern tip of a narrow hilly peninsula that encloses the upper portion of San Diego Bay. For the past several decades, the U.S. Navy has owned most of the surrounding territory and, during the Second World War, a coastal artillery battery occupied the heights. Just north, on State Highway 209, stood another vanished landmark. This was the brightly colored and ornate palace that formerly housed a local school of theosophy. Leave it to the Golden State to mix the military with the metaphysical.

In common with the other purported haunted locations described in this chapter, there is little affirmative evidence to support the notion that the Point Loma Lighthouse is home to a specter. The stories of ghostly infestation seem to rest upon a few anecdotes of disembodied footfalls and moaning voices.

Seri Kassebaum, who worked at the Cabrillo National Monument for five years, was amused by the reports of ghosts at the lighthouse. She is the wife of special effects wizard Kass, who cobbled the fake White Lady of the Elfin Forest. Seri is also a firm skeptic in matters paranormal.

"The Point Loma Lighthouse haunted? Not." Seri paused and laughed. "Not only did I never experience anything even remotely ghost-like, I can't remember even a single instance when it ever came up in conversation among the rangers."

Visitors sometimes had a different view of the lighthouse. Seri recalled that tourists often asked the park staff if the building was haunted. Seri offered her opinion on why the guests were so fixated on ghosts. "It's a 150-year-old building on a remote cliff above the sea. The place is custom made for a ghost story."

The alleged haunting spirit is inexplicably identified as Juan Rodriguez Cabrillo, a Portuguese explorer who sailed under the Spanish flag. Cabrillo led the sea-borne expedition into Alta California and, in September of 1542, discovered San Diego Bay. Ghost legend has it that Cabrillo landed his ships just below the present site of the lighthouse and took personal possession of the peninsula. An abiding avarice for land is cited as the chain that links Cabrillo's spirit to the spot.

Yet anyone acquainted with the geography and history of Point Loma would realize that this story is highly improbable. First, there is no safe harbor in the immediate vicinity of the lighthouse; the cliffs are sheer and rocky. Therefore, Cabrillo's expedition likely made its

POINT LOMA LIGHTHOUSE —PHOTO BY JO CRYDER

landfall further into the bay, near the present-day Ballast Point. The claim that Cabrillo intended to personally homestead the peninsula also runs in the face of historical fact. San Diego was but the first stop in a northward journey along the California coastline. And if Cabrillo had designs on the land, it is certain evidence he was an exceedingly poor judge of real estate. Point Loma was a desolate spot with scant arable land and little water. Unless the explorer meant to take up the life of a fasting and thirsty anchorite, there would be little sense in claiming the peninsula.

The notion that Cabrillo haunts the spot likely comes from the misidentification of the Point Loma Lighthouse as the "Spanish Lighthouse," which apparently began in the late 1890s. The author of the story seems to have been a local entrepreneur known only as Reubin, who conducted tourists on carriage tours to and from the lighthouse. Embellishing history for the entertainment of his clients (and, no doubt, the health of his wallet), Reubin solemnly told his customers that the original Spanish explorers of San Diego had built the lighthouse. And since every old "Spanish" ruin needs a ghost, over the passage of a century, the legend has grown of Cabrillo haunting the beacon.

The earliest written account I could locate alluding to the possibility that the lighthouse was haunted appeared in Herbert Lockwood's book, *Fallout From the Skeleton's Closet*, published in 1967. In this wonderful compendium of odd and engaging anecdotes of San Diego's history, Lockwood tells the story of the Point Loma beacon. The chapter's final paragraph asks rhetorically if the lighthouse was haunted. The author then suggests, tongue firmly in cheek, that if there were a ghost present, it was not Cabrillo's, but the shade of Robert Israel, the former lighthouse keeper.

In my search for witnesses to the phenomena, I was only able to locate one person willing to admit he'd experienced anything uncanny at the lighthouse. Even then, the information was nearly valueless. I'll call my witness Greg, and we met at a used bookshop in San Diego. As our conversation drifted into the subject of local ghosts, I expressed a growing conviction that the Point Loma Lighthouse haunting was a fraud. Greg strenuously objected and declared he had encountered the wraith in 1996. Excited over the prospect of at last finding a witness, I asked Greg to tell me more.

It was at dusk, he said, and he had been enjoying the spectacular view of San Diego Bay from the lighthouse. Then, stepping inside the structure, he suddenly felt a strong invisible presence in the room. This was followed by a blast of chill wind. I waited for the denouement, for surely Greg's eerie preamble would follow with a report of a ghost sighting or some other type of paranormal phenomena. But this was the end of his story. I thanked him for the information and left.

It wasn't that I disbelieved Gregg. He seemed both honest and earnest. Yet the experience was far too subjective to be of measurable worth. Moreover, there was one anomaly to his story. When a cold spot is sensed in a haunted place, the atmosphere is customarily described as motionless and reminiscent of being inside a refrigerator. Seldom is the air reported as being in motion. Therefore, I concluded the blast of chill air was precisely that, a cold breeze. After all, the wind is an almost perpetual element of life at the Point Loma Lighthouse.

It was a warm and spectacularly beautiful day in March 1997 when I visited the lighthouse. The atmosphere was so clear that snow-capped Mount San Gorgonio was visible over a hundred miles away. Out on the Pacific Ocean, the Coronado Islands poked up from the sea like fairy castles.

In speaking with the National Park Service employees, it was soon apparent that they were both amused and weary with the constant assertions of the lighthouse being haunted. Most expressed astonishment that the rumor was in such wide circulation, since none of the staff had ever encountered a ghost or any other supernatural phenomenon.

"The wind blows up here all the time, sometimes with pretty good velocity, and it can make a moaning sound. Maybe that's what caused people to think the lighthouse is haunted," said one park ranger. "Look, I personally believe in the existence of ghosts, but there just aren't any here."

Touring the whitewashed stone tower, I was struck by how lonely the life of lighthouse keeper Robert Israel must have been. Yet I suspect the isolation was more than rewarded by the magnificent views of the bay, mountains, and glittering ocean. The living quarters were snug: four rooms with the doorways now blocked with thick sheets of clear plastic. Climbing up the circular stairway, I entered the greenhouse atmosphere of the beacon room. After only a few moments in the stifling heat, I was praying to encounter a cold spot.

Outside, I noted the presence of a large cistern intended for the collection of rainwater. The barren peninsula isn't endowed with much groundwater, which meant there was no nearby well. Often, when rainfall was scant, water casks were carried to the lighthouse by horse-drawn wagon. Since so many haunted places seem connected to a natural water source, I wondered if the absence of groundwater could be considered a negative factor in determining the likelihood of revenant spirits.

Ultimately, there is little proof that the Point Loma Lighthouse is haunted. Certainly the rangers could be stonewalling regarding the reports of unearthly phenomena, but my sense is that they were telling the truth. As a consequence, I'm inclined to echo Seri Kassebaum's succinct assessment of the ghost: Not.

(The Point Loma Lighthouse is located at the Cabrillo National Monument, which is at the south terminus of California State Route 209, in the City of San Diego. The park is open seven days a week from 9:00 a.m. to 5:15 p.m. There is an admission fee of $5 per car, or $2 for pedestrians, bicyclists and motorcyclists.)

*   *   *

In Richard Senate's fine book, *The Haunted Southland,* is a chapter dedicated to the haunting of the old battlefield at San Pascual. However, the described phenomena were vague and tenuous and, in my opinion, did not constitute sufficient evidence to positively identify the valley as haunted. But one fact cannot be ignored. Throughout history, battlefields from Marathon to Little Big Horn have become known as the homes of unhappy spirits. Therefore, the stories from San Pascual must not be arbitrarily discarded.

Located about 40 miles northeast of downtown San Diego, the San Pascual Valley is a sun-drenched expanse of rolling land marked with green checkerboard squares of avocado trees. This is farming country, but the most prominent landowner is the San Diego Zoo's Wild Animal Park. To the east of the huge game preserve, closer to the rugged foothills, is a State Historical Park that marks the site of the battle.

Little more than a glorified skirmish, the Battle of San Pascual was nonetheless a pivotal event of the Mexican-American War and the largest battle ever fought in California. The ugly little brawl was ostensibly a tactical victory for the *Californios*, but a strategic success for the invading American troops. Had the brave Mexican militia eliminated the small force of Yankee dragoons, they likely would have gone on to retake the entire southern portion of the state from the Americans.

The fight occurred on December 6, 1846, when a weary force of U.S. cavalry emerged from a mountain pass. The Americans, under the command of General Stephen Kearny, were on their way to reinforce the tiny detachment of U.S. Marines holding San Diego. However, in the valley waiting for the Americans was a force of *Californio* horsemen armed with lances, controlled by General Andres Pico.

It was a swirling, disorganized, and savage fight. Although the number of troops engaged was relatively small, the percentage of casualties was high. When evening came, the Americans were in defensive positions on a cacti-covered hillside, with the *Californios* only a short distance away. Five days passed and further combat ensued about five miles to the west, but neither side was strong enough to finish off the other. In time, an American relief column of sailors and marines arrived in the San Pascual Valley and the dragoons were escorted to San Diego.

The published stories about the haunting at San Pascual include scant specific information. The reports of phenomena are maddeningly vague, but include accounts of spectral screams, cold spots, and wispy figures that might be construed as phantom cavalry. As a consequence, there seemed to be two primary avenues of investigation. The first was to interview the San Pascual Park staff. The second required seeking out the local Mexican-American War reenactors who frequent the park, and question them on the haunting.

SAN PASQUAL BATTLEFIELD

Park employees and volunteers were uniformly astonished when I told them the battlefield was listed as a possible haunted site. I learned that nobody among the staff members had ever reported anything even remotely supernatural. The workers also suggested some natural origins for the alleged phenomena.

Their first objection to the stories was that the majority of combat did not occur within the confines of the State Park. The ragged and running fight began on the southern and opposite side of the valley and continued across land currently used for farming. It wasn't until combat ended that the Americans encamped on Mule Hill on the north side of the valley.

"The battle was fought about 500 yards that way," said a ranger, pointing toward a distant green field. "Unless the ghosts are using a public address system, I don't see how you could hear their screams."

But the staffers acknowledged that the reports of spectral cries might be actual auditory events. Just to the west, beyond a ridge is the aforementioned Wild Animal Park. The place is packed with exotic animals, many of which make some fairly extraordinary sounds.

Furthermore, accounts of misty horsemen might be genuine equestrians seen under poor viewing conditions. Farms and horse stables are scattered throughout the neighborhood. As for the cold spots, the battlefield is located near a mountain pass and what could be more natural than random gusts of cool wind? True, the pass leads inland toward the Anza-Borrego Desert, but during the winter, even desert winds can be quite chill.

The historical reenactors I contacted expressed similar sentiments. Many routinely visit the battlefield dressed in uniforms from the 1840s and provide living history displays for visitors. Although most were enormously intrigued by the idea of a haunting at San Pascual, none of the mock troops had ever personally experienced anything uncanny. Nor were they aware of any rumors regarding a ghost.

In fact, I could not locate even a secondhand account of the phantom cavalry at the San Pascual battlefield. As a result, I am presently (and sadly) inclined to believe the ghosts have received their honorable discharges and moved on to their rewards.

(The San Pascual Battlefield is located on California State Route 78, about 1.5 miles east of the city of Escondido and just past the San Diego Zoo's Wild Animal Park. The State Park is open on weekends and there is no admission fee. Historical reenactors annually recreate the engagement on the weekend nearest the battle anniversary.)

*   *   *

So there you have it: three San Diego County haunts of dubious quality. However, the verdict in ghost investigations is almost never irrevocable. Perhaps the reader has visited one of these places and experienced the haunting. If so, I encourage you to write me and share the episode. I'd love nothing better than to redeem the reputations of these allegedly haunted sites.

A BOY'S WILL IS THE WIND'S WILL

Contrary to the excesses of popular literature and the lurid films of Hollywood, the average haunting is anything but spectacular. Almost never does blood drip from walls, nor do ghosts rattle chains or manifest as H.P. Lovecraft monsters. Most often the phenomena are random, harmless, and apparently purposeless. Indeed, the proper attitude in response to ghosts could be pity, for most seem lost and confused. This is particularly true regarding the spirit revenants of children.

I became aware of such a haunting in the fall of 1996. The ghostly sightings and poltergeist activity were occurring in the quiet suburban home of Aprile and Tom. The couple's odd experiences over the past three years have left them convinced their house is occupied by the ghost of a young boy.

Since 1993, they have lived on a broad coastal ridge in the San Diego County community of Encinitas. The history of the region is nearly identical to that of the rest of Southern California. Native Americans of the *Ipai-Diegueno* tribes were the original residents. Then came the Spaniards and the territory became a part of the Rancho Los Encinos land grant. Because water was scarce, both the *Californios* and subsequent American settlers primarily employed the land for cattle grazing. With the arrival of the railroad and, later, a paved coastal highway, the town of Encinitas slowly flourished. Explosive growth occurred in the 1970s and 1980s. By 1995, the community's population had exceeded 50,000 and was still growing. No longer a quiet beach village, the city was a distant suburb of San Diego.

Encinitas is pleasantly schizophrenic. The portion of town hugging the coastline is an archetypal California seaside town from the 1940s. There is a mild bohemian atmosphere. The businesses here are an eclectic mix of coffeehouses, ethnic restaurants, small taverns, metaphysical shops and art galleries. Surfers, merchants, skateboarders, cheerful transients, and joggers crowd the sidewalks. Inland, however, is another and very different Encinitas. This is a land of large housing developments, auto dealerships, and huge shopping centers.

Aprile and Tom enjoy life in Encinitas and operate a small appliance repair service from their home. Both are in their early 40s. Aprile is a vivacious woman who isn't the least bit hesitant to admit she's psychic and has had previous paranormal experiences. Tom is quiet and possessed of a more pragmatic temperament. They make a splendid team but, prior to the spring of 1993, neither suspected they would ever live in a haunted house.

The story began shortly after the couple and Aprile's adult daughter, Tricia, moved into the single-story residence. Built in 1957 and remodeled just prior to their taking possession, the house was in an ideal spot. It was far enough inland to enjoy the sun, yet sufficiently close to the ocean to savor the cool breeze. Aprile loved her new home, but soon noted some odd events.

"Not long after we moved in, I heard the sound of the bedroom closet slamming," Aprile said. "There was nobody in the house at the time and I've got to confess I was a little frightened."

The house was searched, but no culprit was found. As the days followed, the phenomenon was repeated. Tom didn't hear the sounds, but wasn't inordinately surprised. He was used to living with a psychic. Aprile eventually concluded that someone, possibly a ghost, was expressing displeasure over the family's occupancy of the house. But if the spirit's intent was to frighten Aprile into leaving, it failed miserably. She decided to just ignore the boisterous behavior, for she was not going to be driven from her new home. The tactic seemed to work, because the doors soon ceased to slam shut.

Not long afterward, however, Aprile began to catch sight of gliding movement in her peripheral vision. Again and again, she would see a shape of a small person, but when she turned to examine the figure, it vanished. These incidents occurred at various locations throughout the house and Aprile developed the strong feeling that an invisible guest was monitoring her movements.

"It wasn't frightening, because by then I realized it was just interested in what I was doing," she said.

Then came the morning when Aprile finally saw the apparition. She was walking down the hallway toward the living room when she observed a young boy. He appeared to be about 6 years old, with a swarthy complexion and dark hair. The child wore a distinctive shirt that bore a multi-colored design, reminding Aprile of a quilt. For a moment she and the child simply watched each other. Then the boy vanished.

"When I first saw him, he looked so real I thought he was a neighborhood kid. I wondered if maybe he'd gotten lost and come into my house. But when he disappeared, I realized he was our ghost," she said.

The corporeal appearance of the specter is a little-known element of ghost reports. Indeed, the popular belief is that all ghosts are luminescent and transparent; and float through the air, staring mournfully at observers. But that isn't necessarily so. Many apparitions possess a tangible and concrete form and can behave as any other human being. Moreover, the actions of such a ghost can conform to physical laws and the surrounding environment. Often it is only the ghost's anachronistic clothing or sudden disappearance that alerts the witness to the supernatural aspect of the sighting. In fact, it is altogether possible that many of us have encountered this variety of apparition without ever suspecting its true nature.

In the following weeks, Aprile saw the boy several more times and on each occasion the specter always appeared fully physical. Sometimes the child was simply wandering through the house. In other instances, he seemed to briefly visit with Aprile. There was never any overt communication, but she sensed that the meetings were interactive. The phantasm appeared to be aware of her presence and clearly wished to be seen. Before long, Aprile realized the unearthly child was lonely and had "adopted" the human family.

When she told Tom and Tricia of the ghostly experiences, they were polite but clearly unconvinced. It was one thing to acknowledge the potential existence of psychic phenomena and quite another to admit they had a ghost in residence. Aprile wasn't disturbed by their attitude, for she suspected that, in time, they too would meet the boy. She was right.

Tricia was the next person to see the child. One afternoon, when she was alone in the house, she entered the living room and saw the boy. Consistent with Aprile's encounters, the ghost bore every appearance of being physically real. Thinking the child had wandered in from the neighborhood, Tricia went to see if she could help him. But the boy vanished before her eyes. The young woman was stunned and stared at the empty spot. A second later, she saw the child reappear several yards away. The phantom was crouched beneath the dining room table, his eyes merry and riveted on the woman. By now Tricia realized she'd met the ghost.

Intrigued, Tricia again moved toward the wraith and he disappeared once more. Turning, she next saw the boy in the kitchen. The ghost stared at her and then vanished a final time.

"Tricia and I compared notes on what she'd seen," Aprile explained. The boy was wearing that strange shirt and looked identical to how I'd seen him. We both felt the boy was playing with Tricia. You know, like a game of tag."

Both Tricia and Aprile's encounters contained the unmistakable features marking them as interactive. The apparition behaved not as an insensate video image, but as a playful child. For Aprile, her daughter's experience was strong corroborative evidence that they were dealing with a sentient, albeit immature, entity.

Tom, however, remained quietly skeptical; there were no such things as ghosts.

Then two events occurred that forced him to reassess his view.

The first happened one afternoon as Tom approached the empty house. As he inserted the key into the door lock, he was suddenly aware of a noise from inside the home. Listening closely, he heard a collection of buzzing, indistinct voices from within. It was, thought Tom, almost like the sound of a party.

Realizing that Aprile and Tricia weren't home, Tom wondered if he hadn't interrupted burglars in the process of pillaging his home. But if that were the case, they were noisiest criminals in history. Tom cocked an ear toward the door, hoping to make some sense of the muddled conversation, but the words remained maddeningly blurred. Finally, Tom threw open the door, fully expecting to see someone inside. But the living room was empty and the voices instantly ceased. Puzzled and a little apprehensive, Tom stood in the doorway, for he now had the uncanny sense he had disturbed some type of invisible meeting. He checked the rest of the house and found it vacant.

Although Tom did not know it, this kind of auditory episode is a routine form of ghost and poltergeist manifestation. Witnesses hear the gabble of blurred conversation from an empty room, yet words and phrases cannot be deciphered. A few people have even described the phenomenon as sounding like a distant party. Furthermore, witnesses almost always report the sound stops abruptly when they enter the room.

Not long afterward, Tom had his first and only visual encounter with the ghost. It was late afternoon and he was walking down the hallway when he stopped short in his tracks. Approaching him was a small boy wearing a quilt-like shirt. In Tom's instance, however, the apparition appeared more conventionally "ghost-like," being translucent and somewhat indistinct. The child then vanished.

It is worthwhile to note the differences in how the apparition was perceived by the various family members. Unless the ghost possessed the conscious ability to change its appearance, this disparity suggests that the observers played significant roles in how the ghost was sensed. In essence, because Tom may have been culturally conditioned to expect a ghost would appear as an opaque figure, this was how he saw the spirit. Some researchers posit that a ghost sighting is not a function of physical vision, but a telepathic operation of the observer's mind. The ghost encounter, therefore, involves two distinct functions: the ethereal stimuli and the percipient witness, who exercises some type of subconscious control over how the ghost phenomenon is deciphered.

Tom shared his experiences with Aprile and conceded that there was a ghost in the house. By now, all three adults were on the lookout for the spirit, but this was one of the last occasions the spectral child was seen. The last visual encounter occurred in 1993, but other events make it clear that the ghost was still in residence. One indicator was in the behavior of the family pets. Aprile and Tom own two cats and both developed a habit of watching an invisible person move through the house. The felines don't seem threatened or frightened by the entity, simply interested.

"It's really kind of eerie," said Aprile. "Both cats will begin staring at a spot and then track movement through the room. We never see anything, but they sure do."

Another type of manifestation in the household is consistent with classic poltergeist phenomenon. At various times, small personal items and tools have disappeared, only to be found later in strange locations. In particular, the ghost seems to enjoy hiding Tom's tools. On one occasion, Tom placed an electric sander on a nearby work bench, but when he turned to pick the appliance up, it was gone. He was perplexed and searched the garage thoroughly, but could not find the tool. Several days later, however, he discovered the sander inside a microwave oven he was repairing. On another occasion, some important papers were missing for several days. After conducting a prolonged search of every nook and cranny of the house, Aprile discovered the documents lying in plain sight.

The phenomenon is sometimes annoying, but Aprile takes it with a grain of salt. "He's a lonely little guy and just wants to play."

The unearthly boy may also be interested in other kinds of modern electronic equipment. Like most business owners, Aprile and Tom have a facsimile machine in their home. It is a handy device and often invaluable. Yet throughout much of 1996, the family received a series of phantom calls on the facsimile. With almost clockwork regularity, the telephone line dedicated to the fax would ring at 7:00 p.m. The call was automatically answered and, seconds later the machine ejected a blank sheet of paper. No message was ever received.

At first, Tom and Aprile dismissed the calls as the work of a human prankster. But the phenomenon continued sporadically over a year's time, with the telephone always ringing at 7:00 p.m. If this was the product of a human practical joker, thought Aprile, the guy was both diligent and singularly unimaginative. Eventually, she began to suspect the ghost was producing the calls. Perhaps the device fascinated the specter; most little boys find buzzing, light-festooned machines irresistible. Yet Aprile could never fathom the apparent importance of the time of the calls.

"If it was the ghost using the telephone," wondered Aprile, "how did he know it was seven o'clock? Did he see the clock?"

Indeed, how does a phantom tell time?

In only one instance has Aprile physically felt the ghost. This occurred in 1996 while she was in the kitchen washing dishes. Suddenly, she felt a distinct tug on her jeans. Thinking that perhaps Tom had slipped into the house, she quickly turned around, but saw no one. Later, she concluded the ghostly child simply wanted some attention.

Aprile has some notions regarding the origin of the spirit. She feels that the boy lived and died in the area and entered the house seeking refuge from a world he does not understand. The slamming of the closet doors, believes Aprile, was a defense mechanism. Initially wary and unhappy over the new tenants, the ghost made the noises to express his dissatisfaction and perhaps frighten off the intruders. In time, however, the specter has apparently grown to like the family. Aprile senses the boy has adopted her and Tom as surrogate parents. Alone and confused over his own death, the child seeks the company of the living. Because of this, Aprile strives to be accommodating.

"More than anything, I feel sorry for the little guy." Aprile's voice was slightly sad.

Her story made me wonder how long the ghost had been in residence. The previous owners had apparently never mentioned the phenomena. This could have been a deliberate attempt to conceal the haunting, but it was just as likely the former occupants had experienced nothing uncanny. Then I remembered an important element in Aprile's account: there was a major remodeling job completed on the house just prior to the family taking possession.

Many ghost researchers have noted an apparent connection between the structural renovation of a house and the subsequent appearance of a ghost. We can only dimly comprehend why a wraith would object to the physical alteration of a building. Perhaps when humans shift corporeal walls, they also cause a collateral change in energy matrices on several planes of reality.

This is a dim and overly simplistic echo of the theory underlying the Chinese art of geomancy known as *Feng Shui*. At the risk of oversimplification, *Feng Shui* adherents believe that by altering the floor plan of a building, the flow of spiritual energy can be either strengthened or impeded. Therefore, physical changes in a structure might actually discomfit ethereal beings. At the same time, it's possible the poltergeist response to remodeling might be borne of a ghost's irrational sense of proprietorship or even simple aesthetics.

My interview with Aprile completed, I began some historical research on both the neighborhood and the child. The home is built a short distance from the former site of a seasonal lake or pond. The small pool was filled in when the region was prepared for residential development. In the 1870s, the land was part of the MacKinnon Ranch. Cattle were grazed on the hills and there was some limited farming. Hector MacKinnon was a Civil War veteran from Ohio and his original home was nowhere near the site, so it didn't seem likely the child was from that family. Yet this does not rule out the possibility that tenant farmers had lived near the place.

When I spoke with a local historian, she suggested the wraith might be of Native American or Mexican heritage. Certainly the swarthy complexion, dark hair, and clothing were suggestive of such an early resident. Yet Aprile was reluctant to identify the child as a member of either group. Another regional history enthusiast alerted me to the legend that an old Native American burial ground may have overlooked the nearby Batiquitos Lagoon. But the information did not seem to apply to the haunting, for the marshy inlet was over a mile from Aprile's home, a sizeable distance for a ghost to wander. In the end, the identity of the child may never be known.

The most intriguing aspect of the haunting was the poltergeist element. This was because none of the family appeared to be a member of the poltergeist "carrier" group. Researchers have identified several types of people who seem to provide the raw materials for physical phenomena. They include adolescents and the victims of *grand mal* epileptic seizures.

The modern paranormal research community generally eschews the term "poltergeist" in favor of "Recurring Spontaneous Psycho-Kinetic" activity, or RSPK. (And, semantically speaking, the latter term is incredible, for it isn't often that English can be made to sound more curt and multisyllabic than German.) Observers of RSPK phenomena conjecture that the stress of puberty can have a hidden impact on children.

Often the adolescent years are marked by rebellious behavior as the youth begins to assert his or her budding status as a functioning adult. This period of tumultuous change may also provoke the development of psychokinetic energy within the teen. At times this surging power can manifest in noisy and destructive ways. Loud raps are heard on walls, light bulbs are shattered, electric appliances malfunction or operate independent of human control. Parapsychologists believe this activity is subconsciously created by the youth, who may be as frightened by the violent episodes as everyone else. Researchers argue that the poltergeist is not a ghost, but merely a form of unexplained human ability.

Yet no such "target" RSPK generators were present in Aprile's home, so this theory does not seem to apply. Rather, we must accept the strong possibility that the events were being generated by an independent entity. But was this a ghost or something far different? Some more unorthodox paranormal researchers have connected poltergeist phenomena with a species of ethereal creature known as an "elemental." These investigators suggest that elementals might be the motivating intelligence behind many outbreaks of poltergeist activity.

Throughout recorded history and all around the globe, mankind has reported encounters with fairies, elves, the little people, and water sprites. The Hindus refer to such spirits as *devas* and *asuras*. Hawaiians call them *e'epa* and *menehune*. In Ireland, they are the famous leprechaun and the *Tuatha de Danaan*. One theory is that these entities are a variety of nature spirits that are only occasionally visible to humans. In general, elementals appear to possess only limited intelligence and their behavior is marked by extreme capriciousness. They can be helpful or malicious, depending on their highly changeable mood. Finally, these creatures may be endowed with a capacity to temporarily assume human or animal form.

Now the very notion of an empirical belief in fairies might sound slightly deranged to modern ears, but such keen intellects as Arthur Conan Doyle and W.Y. Evans-Wentz, a scholar who invested years of study into the phenomena, felt there was compelling testimonial evidence for such creatures. What's more, when stripped of the fairy-tale format, the ancient stories of household sprites are in many ways akin to modern poltergeist reports. Indeed, with the exception of the brief spate of apparitions, the events occurring in the Encinitas home strongly resemble the traditional legends of a playful sprite or elf. A ridiculous notion? Perhaps, but I mention this theory to illustrate one vital fact: the origins of ghost phenomena may be far stranger than we can comprehend.

Fortunately, Aprile isn't overly concerned whether the resident entity is a poltergeist, elemental, or friendly ghost. She is content to provide an earthly home for the wraith, so long as the young spook minds its manners.

A GENTLE
HAUNTING

Many people carry the erroneous belief that the diabolic (and fraudulent) antics of the ghosts from the *Amityville Horror* are par for the spectral course. Indeed, mention of the word poltergeist can provoke a shiver from the listener. But this is not the case as can be seen from the next story.

The suburban house was one of thousands scattered across the eastern portion of Carlsbad. It sat on Chestnut Avenue on a bald coastal hill about two miles from the ocean. With its neatly mown lawn and freshly trimmed shrubs, there was little to distinguish the structure from its neighbors. Yet from 1975 through at least 1984, the house was occupied by a discreet and strangely comforting spectral presence.

Is this an odd way to describe a poltergeist? Perhaps, but the family who encountered the spirit wasn't typical either. Rather than react with irrational fear and panic, they simply adjusted their views on the nature of life and accommodated themselves to the specter. What follows is the brief history of a peaceful poltergeist and its relationship with a mature and sensible family.

I first learned of this haunting through a mutual friend. It was precisely the type of account a ghost researcher relishes: a previously unreported haunting. The former homeowner's name was Ann Marie Helmut and, after less than five minutes of conversation, I found myself liking the cheerful woman. Although she initially expressed serious doubts her strange story was even worthy of telling, she eventually acceded to my request.

As she recounted her tale, I grew increasingly impressed with Ann Marie's attitude. It was she who set the tenor for how her children would react to the supernatural phenomena occurring in their home. Her unruffled response to the ghost can be attributed to the fact Ann Marie was no stranger to phantom encounters.

She described a childhood experience when she and her family took up temporary residence in Sweden. "It was 1949 and we had just moved into an old one-room house. It was very primitive, especially for a family fresh from the United States. Not long after we were settled, we all began to hear the sound of sobbing."

Initially, Ann Marie and her parents were taken aback by the eerie sounds. Night after night, the cabin would throb with the heartbreaking wail of crying women. But after a time, the auditory events became so common, the family accepted the sounds without much excitement. They subsequently learned that, many years previous, a double suicide had occurred in the house. The victims were a pair of middle-aged unmarried sisters who had hung themselves.

As a young witness to the doleful phenomena, Ann Marie developed a tolerant attitude toward matters paranormal. "Once you get over being startled, there really isn't anything to be frightened of," she said. "These things can't hurt us and I grew to feel very sorry for the two sisters."

Still, Ann Marie never suspected that one day she would be living in another haunted house.

In 1975, while on a house-hunting expedition in Carlsbad, Ann Marie and her three children spotted the Chestnut Avenue residence. The house seemed perfect for their needs and she made an offer. Ann Marie also learned a curious fact about the sellers. They were a middle-aged couple who had expressed an undefined but powerful dislike for the house. They had only lived there for a brief time and wanted out quickly. Ann Marie could not discover the reason for the couple's dissatisfaction, but in time the answer became obvious.

From the beginning Ann Marie was attracted to the residence and always sensed a welcoming atmosphere. She and her children moved in and soon converted the house into a bustling, happy home. The kids rapidly made friends and all seemed quite normal. Before long, however, some odd things began to happen. Both Ann Marie and the children repeatedly caught glimpses of a tenuous misty shape gliding through the living room, hallway, and den. Ann Marie likened the apparition to a "blob" of foggy shadow. At first no one spoke of the nebulous intruder, but finally Ann Marie and the kids confirmed each other's observations. They'd all seen the shape, but nobody felt threatened by the presence.

Nonetheless, for a time Ann Marie studiously attempted to dismiss her observations as a trick of the eye.

"I'd be working in the kitchen and, from the corner of my eye, I'd see a person-shaped shadow slip down the hall," she explained. "But you'd turn and the image would be gone. After awhile I accepted the fact that something or someone was in the house."

Shortly thereafter, strange events began occurring overnight in the kitchen. The toaster, blender, and other electrical appliances began to operate of their own volition. Then the cupboard doors and drawers began to open by themselves. Before going to bed, Ann Marie would routinely ensure the kitchen was closed up and tidy. Yet frequently the drawers and cupboards were found wide open in the morning. It was as if a nocturnal visitor was puttering in the kitchen.

"I can remember lying in bed and suddenly hearing the blender start up, or sometimes the dishwasher," she said. "At first I thought it might have been one of the kids playing a game. But they were either asleep or heard it themselves."

By this time Ann Marie had reached the conclusion that there was a ghost in the house. Still, she wasn't inordinately disturbed by the fact. "If the house was haunted, it was by a pleasant spirit. It simply wasn't worth worrying about."

The kitchen phenomena continued intermittently for nine years. Yet Ann Marie refused to become frightened. Instead, she would shut the appliance off and genially ask the entity to stop the nonsense. After all, she worked for a living and needed her sleep. The ghost was unfailingly compliant and, for at least a few days, the kitchen would be quiet.

Clearly interested in modern electronics, the invisible lodger next initiated experiments with another device. This was the television in the den, which began to demonstrate a mind of its own. Indeed the Helmut household's poltergeist behaved as so many of its breed. They seem attracted to electrically operated equipment and often play with them. The behavior could be sparked by simple curiosity or perhaps the powered appliances have an impact on the poltergeist's invisible plane of existence.

"We'd be sitting watching TV when the station would suddenly switch to Channel 11. Always Channel 11. We could never figure out the significance of that," Ann Marie said with a puzzled tone. "And we didn't have a remote control, so you had to get up and physically change the channel."

Visitors too witnessed this phenomenon. Ann Marie told of the time when a relative from Colorado came to visit. "She was watching TV in the den when the channel changed. At the same time, she mentioned feeling very cold. Freezer cold. From that time onward she wouldn't stay in that room by herself."

Ann Marie had also felt the cold spot in the den and was silently grateful for independent corroboration of the sensation. The small area of coolness was only detectable during nighttime hours and seemed confined to a spot near the interior south wall.

"It didn't make any difference whether it was summer or winter. When the sun went down, the air in that one place became cooler than anywhere else in the house," said Ann Marie.

Another recurring event took place in the den. "I would be sitting watching television when suddenly there'd be the overpowering feeling of someone standing beside me. Of course, I'd look and there was nobody there."

Ann Marie, however, did not panic.

"At first I was a little upset, but then I realized he was simply interested in what I was doing," said Ann Marie. "So I turned to where I thought he was standing and asked him what he wanted. After that, he'd usually move on."

Ann Marie's statement caused me to ask how she knew the entity was male.

"Oh, it was definitely a masculine presence. You could just feel it," she replied. "Both the kids and I were in agreement on that."

Some evidence of the ghost's gender and identity was offered in the following months. One evening, Ann Marie had taken a shower and filled the bathroom with steam. As she dried off, her attention was drawn to the mist-shrouded mirror. There, in profile, was the face of a Native American male. Ann Marie gaped at the vision and then called her children into the bathroom. They too saw the man's face.

"My first reaction was that it was simply a random image on the glass, possibly caused by dust and the steam," said Ann Marie. "But at the same time, I'd never seen anything quite like it. The face was quite distinct."

Ann Marie attacked the mirror with window cleaner and a rag, polishing the glass until it was spotless. But in the following months the misty image of the Indian returned on several occasions and was seen by all members of the family. There was never any sense that they were actually seeing the animate face of a spirit, explained Ann Marie. Rather, it was as if a spectral portrait was being sporadically offered to the family.

One other member of the family was affected by the specter's presence. This was the family dog, a huge Great Dane. Ordinarily, dogs react with ferocity or terror when in proximity to a ghost, yet this was not the case in the Helmut household. The enormous dog would merely become alert and begin to watch an invisible person as it moved through the room. The Great Dane never seemed frightened of the phantasm, simply interested.

As the years passed, the Helmut family grew increasingly accustomed to their unseen lodger. When neighborhood kids slept over, Ann Marie would casually tell them not to be concerned if they heard or saw anything strange. It was simply the ghost and no cause for anxiety. In fact, Ann Marie grew to appreciate the incorporeal presence. She felt that the beneficent spirit was watching over the house and her family. When it came time for them to move in 1984, Ann Marie genuinely regretted leaving the phantom behind, for he had been a silent and invisible friend.

"I always had the sense that nothing bad could happen while he was watching over the house," Ann Marie said quietly. "He liked us and I always had the feeling we were protected."

But who was the unearthly watchman?

Historical research on the house revealed very little. Carlsbad city records indicated it was built in 1965 as part of a large tract of homes. With the exception of the installation of a paved patio, no significant alterations were made to the residence. Prior to construction of the house, the hillside was vacant and possibly used for cattle grazing in the nineteenth century. But did Native Americans live on the land before the Spanish and Americans arrived?

Known today as the *Luiseno* Indians, a name given the tribe by the San Luis Rey Mission priests, the original inhabitants of Carlsbad were of Shoshone extraction. In their own language, the tribes living along the coastline were called *Payamkuchum*. A hunter-gatherer culture, the *Payamkuchum* were a spiritual people who lived in concordance with their environment.

Most often, the *Payamkuchum* dwelt in villages near tidal inlets or watercourses. The present location of the house is about an equal distance from the Buena Vista and Agua Hedionda lagoons. The latter location is significant. In 1769, Spanish explorers found a deserted Indian settlement on the banks of the marshy cove. Therefore, it is possible a village could have existed near the present site of the house.

Similarly, might a Native American burial ground be located nearby? Here the issue becomes a little obscure. Some anthropologists claim the prevailing funeral custom among the Native Americans in this area of Southern California was cremation. Others assert that bodies were buried near tidal inlets. Regardless, there is no information to suggest that the homebuilders ever uncovered human remains while developing the housing tract.

Yes, it is true that the discovery of bodies at construction sites have been deliberately overlooked in the past. But based on the gentle behavior of the wraith, the violated graveyard scenario appears improbable. Such hauntings are endowed with the unmistakable flavor of ill will, very different from the placid spirit in the Helmut house.

One salient question regarding the phenomena is whether it was simply a "routine" outbreak of poltergeist activity. If so, the presence of teenagers in the Helmut household is enormously important. As research has repeatedly demonstrated, pubescent children and teens are often the generators of poltergeist phenomena. Or, as other observers have postulated, incorporeal entities may access the energy of youthful humans in order to make themselves manifest. But in the instance of the Helmuts, the events were never violent or destructive. This implies the Helmut children were both happy and emotionally healthy, and therefore unlikely to be producing the paranormal episodes.

Ann Marie Helmut and her family experienced some incredible things. Had they been predisposed to fear and panic, their lives could easily have been changed into a world of terror. For it seems that when humans choose to be "victims," the poltergeist will happily embrace the role of persecutor. In this instance, however, the family took the eerie happenings in stride.

"Life is very short, so you have to remain open to every amazing thing that happens. If you refuse to become afraid, you can experience some pretty incredible things," Ann Marie said.

Hotel Del Coronado —Photo By Jo Cryder

COINAGE OF THE BRAIN: THE HOTEL DEL CORONADO

Over much of the past century, the Hotel Del Coronado has maintained a reputation as one of America's most famous haunted buildings. This is indeed remarkable, since the majority of alleged ghost encounters in the sprawling hotel remain largely vague and apocryphal. Please understand I'm not suggesting the San Diego County landmark isn't haunted, but the spirits may not be ghosts as we understand the generic term.

Before discussing the nature of the phenomena, however, let us briefly examine the history of the ornate Victorian structure. In 1886, San Diego businessmen Elisha S. Babcock and H.L. Story were hunting rabbit in Coronado. At that time, Coronado was a wild and lonely peninsula of sandy beaches and dense underbrush. Yet Babcock and Story found themselves envisioning a world-class resort at the isolated site. The land was purchased and construction began soon afterward. By 1888, the Hotel Del Coronado was open for business and soon attained prominence as one of the premier hotels in the country.

Since then the flamboyant building has been host to over a century's worth of American celebrities. Presidents, film stars, and foreign dignitaries have all enjoyed the luxury, charm, and service of "the Del," as it is locally called. In recent years, Presidents Reagan and Clinton continued this tradition by staying at the hotel. In addition, the hotel has been the setting for several motion pictures including *Some Like it Hot*.

At the risk of sounding like an utter shill for the Del, no trip to San Diego is complete without at least a cursory inspection of the hotel. The lobby is a splendid wilderness of dark wood paneling that recalls an era of Victorian opulence. My favorite time of year to visit the Del is Christmas, when a huge decorated tree dominates the lobby.

The purported origin of the haunting of the hotel arose from an event occurring in 1892. The basic elements of the story are as follows: in late November a woman who has since been tentatively identified as Kate Morgan checked into the hotel under the alias of Lottie Anderson Bernard. Popular legend has it the woman was pregnant and had just been abandoned by her rakish husband. A few days after taking up lodgings, Kate was found dead outside the hotel, on the stairway leading to the beach. She had sustained a single gunshot wound to the head. A .44 caliber revolver was found near her body.

A coroner's inquest was conducted. Witnesses reported that in the days prior to her death, the mystery woman had been anxious and morose. Others said the victim complained of suffering from stomach cancer, but a local physician wondered if the symptoms weren't more consistent with pregnancy. Finally, a San Diego gun shop owner recalled that Kate had purchased a large caliber revolver only a short time before her body was found. The cause of death was determined to be suicide and the sad woman was subsequently buried in Mount Hope Cemetery in San Diego.

Here, both the alleged haunting and confusion begin.

Not long after the discovery of the suicide victim, reports began to circulate of poltergeist activity in Room 502, which corresponds with the present Room 3502. It was popularly thought for a long time that this was the room occupied by Kate prior to her death. Not surprisingly, the two "facts" were connected and a haunting was born.

Yet attorney Alan M. May, in his alternately useful and peculiar book, *The Legend of Kate Morgan: The Hunt for the Haunt of the Hotel Del Coronado*, conclusively demonstrated that Kate was actually housed in Room 302, now known as Room 3312. Room 3502, it was revealed, was likely a maid's quarters.

(One final word on May's strange book before proceeding, however. It was May who apparently initiated stories about a ghostly face seen on a television screen in Room 3312. In addition, he asserted that he enjoyed a Thanksgiving dinner with the ghostly Kate, who incredibly, drank champagne. The spirit confirmed May's theory that she did not commit suicide, but was murdered. Finally, May strongly suggested that he was a long-lost descendent of Kate Morgan. In my somewhat harsh opinion, elements of the book are either over-wrought fiction, or evidence that May was utterly obsessed with the ghost.)

Through the years, paranormal occurrences have been reported in both Rooms 3502 and 3312. Room 3502 has been the scene of typical low-grade poltergeist phenomena: lights flicker, small items are moved, the curtains billow, and a spectral illumination has been allegedly seen. Similarly, Room 3312 has exhibited some mindless events: lights malfunction, Alan May allegedly saw Kate's face on the television screen, and the window screens have reportedly fallen off. In both rooms, guests and hotel employees have also mentioned the sensation of being watched by an unseen presence.

It is possible the spirit of Kate Morgan does linger at the site. Many researchers have noted that suicide victims are often prime candidates to become ghosts. Yet the fact is that the "ghostly" incidents described in the majority of published material on the famous haunting of the hotel are innocuous. If the episodes occurred in the average home, they would likely be casually dismissed. Indeed, when compared against the spectral phenomena reported at La Casa de Estudillo or the Whaley House, the Hotel Del Coronado's ghost is a phantasmagoric underachiever.

So why has the ghostly reputation of the resort flourished for nearly a century?

I have a theory.

We begin with a tragedy, in this instance, the suicide of a mystery woman. The elements of Kate's lonely death could be considered ludicrously melodramatic, were they not true and profoundly sad. Under an alias, a pregnant woman secures lodgings in one of the most exclusive hotels in Southern California. Terrified and anguished at the thought of being abandoned by a ne'er-do-well

HOTEL DEL CORONADO —PHOTO BY JO CRYDER

husband, she waits in vain for his arrival. After a few days, she may have attempted to abort the fetus, but was unsuccessful. Finally, the forsaken woman buys a gun. The next evening, overlooking the sea, the despairing lady places the gun to her head and ends her life.

Not surprisingly, the death excited some considerable attention throughout the hotel and nearby San Diego. Most human beings love to gossip and we can naturally presume the suicide was the primary topic of discussion among the resort staff for quite some time. After all, they were ancillary participants in the lurid and fatal drama. At this point, all it took was for one employee to claim that they had encountered a paranormal event and the kindling would have been ignited. Maybe it was something as ordinary as a curtain billowing in consequence of a low-lying draft, or a light flickering unexpectedly. It made no difference whether the initiating episode was caused by a ghost or of utterly mundane origin. Once told, the story of the haunting would have spread like wildfire.

This was the late Victorian era and there was an enormous interest in Spiritualism, ghost photography, and communication with the dead. It was the epoch of renowned mediums Lenora Piper and Eusapia Palladio, who seemed to offer strong and comforting evidence of the existence of life after death. Ghosts were imagined to be everywhere.

Now as the ghost story came to the attention of the Hotel Del Coronado's management, they likely would have acted swiftly to quash the strange rumors. (This was in a time, remember, before ghosts were considered a canny marketing device.) Perhaps, in an effort to obscure the story, the managers deliberately tried to conceal the location of the suicide victim's lodgings. It is only a theory, but this might account for the subsequent confusion between Rooms 302 and 502. Further blurring of the location probably happened when the rooms were renumbered.

Yet the haunting refused to die. Decade after decade, old employees may have passed the original ghost story on to new workers as a form of hazing, and with each telling the accounts were increasingly embellished. And there could be another reason why the tale has persisted and grown. Work, even in a place as glamorous as the Hotel Del Coronado, is generally boring. The chilling stories may well have been an unintentional means of injecting a little drama and excitement into otherwise tedious labor. In time, some staff members may have been predisposed to attribute any curious occurrence in the rooms to being the agency of spooks.

Guests may also have played an essential role in the creation of the haunting. Many were aware of the alleged weird events, often through stories circulated in books on ghost phenomena. Some people visited for the expressed purpose of occupying the haunted room (whichever one it might be) and their preexisting beliefs in the validity of the ghost provided an impetus to identify any event, however commonplace, as evidence of spectral infestation.

Over the years, the legend of the haunting of the Hotel Del Coronado became a well-established "fact." Yet nobody, with the exception of Alan May, has reported seeing an apparition of the unfortunate Kate. Furthermore, the "ghostly" manifestations remain maddeningly equivocal. In fairness, there are anecdotal accounts of other ghosts seen in the hotel. These include a waltzing Victorian lady and the shade of a former gardener. But Kate has been a no-show. In fact, the number of apparitions reported seen in the Hotel Del Coronado is miniscule compared with other haunted places.

Still, there may indeed be spirits in the hotel, but they may be phantoms of our own creation.

I'm not referring to hallucinations or imagination gone wild, but genuine spooks that we have carelessly spawned. In Tibetan Buddhist theology such a creature is known as a *tulpa*. Crudely stated, the Buddhist belief is that everything in existence began with a thought or mental visualization. This was how God created the universe. Human beings too possess this awesome ability to create, but most cannot consciously employ the gift. This, however, does not mean we don't senselessly and randomly utilize that power to bring life forms into reality.

In essence, many ghosts might be the progeny of the unwitting human mind. Apply that theory to the "haunting" of the Hotel Del Coronado.

For nearly one hundred years, guests and employees of the resort have engaged in thought and reflection regarding the resident "ghost." (And even the skeptic must invest some consideration before resolving to disbelieve in the spirit.) That aggregate reservoir of mental energy didn't evaporate. Every thought rides on an electrical current and it is a law of physics that energy cannot be destroyed. Therefore, a century of belief in the "haunted" hotel has produced the genuine artificial article.

(And while I'm bashing famous spectral places, I might as well state that I think a similar dynamic has created the ambiguous and nebulous phenomena of the notorious Winchester House in San Jose, California.)

Some tangential but strong evidence to support this theory of the ability of humans to produce ghost phenomena can be derived from a startling series of experiments conducted in Canada in the 1970s.

Under the direction of A.R.G. and Iris Owen, eight members of the Toronto Society for Psychical Research endeavored to create an artificial ghost. The team developed a fictional seventeenth-century Englishman named Philip and provided him with an equally spurious personal history. Experiment participants concentrated on the imaginary Philip and conducted seances in hopes of contacting the manufactured spirit.

After several months of effort, the séance group was able to obtain psychokinetic phenomena that purportedly emanated from Philip. They included table-tipping, audible raps and, eventually, some slight levitation. Employing those raps in a primitive code, the group elicited answers from Philip that confirmed the elements of his fictional history. Philip communicated with the group for nearly three years and the Toronto researchers went on to create other ersatz entities. The Canadians had clearly demonstrated it was possible to construct a ghost.

If eight people over a period of months can manufacture a ghost, complete with physical manifestations and the appearance of consciousness, what then could be accomplished by thousands of people, over the course of an entire century, unthinkingly engaged in the same task? Indeed, I'm amazed the Hotel Del Coronado isn't packed to the rafters with artificial phantoms.

Could it be possible to invent a modern resident ghost at the hotel? At the risk of recklessness, I'm going to conduct my own ghost manufacturing experiment and, in the next paragraph, will endeavor to the lay the foundation for an entirely false Hotel Del Coronado ghost.

Kids, don't try this at home!

Like many U.S. presidents, Richard M. Nixon was a guest of the hotel. A native Californian, Nixon had an affinity for seaside resorts, as made evident by his famous western White House in San Clemente. So, might it be possible that the revenant spirit of Nixon still wanders the interior courtyard of the Hotel Del Coronado, perhaps recalling happier days?

Please, please, please remember that the above paragraph is

not true and intended only as a test. If, however, in ten years' time, stories are in circulation that the meandering wraith of Tricky Dick has been seen at the Del, you'll know where the story started.

Irrespective of the origin of the phenomena, the Hotel Del Coronado is certain to maintain its celebrity as one of America's foremost haunted places. Reports on the insignificant "ghost" episodes will continue to surface and the garbled story of poor Kate will be offered as an explanation for the haunting. Yet the episodes occurring within the hotel may possess a far greater meaning. For if the ghosts are the coinage of our own psyche, it could constitute provocative evidence of the incredible and unsuspected powers of the human mind.

GUESS WHO'S COMING TO DINNER?

The Hunter Steakhouse sits on a grassy bluff just above sedate waters of the Buena Vista Lagoon in Oceanside. It is a scenic spot for an eatery: the broad lagoon is home to a wild bird sanctuary and, less than a mile to the west, the Pacific Ocean sparkles. In the opposite direction, the view extends inland to the rugged coastal mountains. When the mist is heavy, the lagoon is endowed with a dreamscape quality. But there is more than fine scenery to recommend the Hunter, for the food is wonderful and service marvelously attentive.

One final and minor note must be added. The Hunter Steakhouse is apparently haunted.

The dim genesis of this ghost investigation occurred in early 1982, while I was working as a young patrol officer with the Oceanside Police Department. Fifteen years passed before I finally began to solicit information on the haunting. Luckily, during that intervening period, the unearthly phenomena were ongoing.

Back in 1982, however, I was working the graveyard shift. My partner and I were dispatched to handle a burglar alarm activation at the restaurant, which was then known as the Hungry Hunter. (In 1996 the business underwent a name change.) It was well after midnight and the restaurant was deserted. Shining our flashlights, we checked the exterior for signs of a break-in, but the building was secure.

Later, we stood in the empty parking lot, waiting for the owner to arrive. My partner puffed on a cigarette and quietly told me of the rumors that the restaurant was haunted. Although the veteran officer hadn't actually seen anything himself, he had heard stories about apparitions and poltergeist activity inside the building. Furthermore, the restaurant's alarm system activated on an almost regular basis, something he and the other cops found strange because no forced entry was ever found. He added one final piece of macabre information: the restaurant was built on top of an old cemetery.

I listened in silence thinking I was the victim of a spooky practical joke. After all, I had just transferred to the Oceanside Police Department and it is a law enforcement tradition for veteran officers to haze their younger counterparts. But I soon realized my compatriot was deadly serious. With no small amount of scorn, I laughed the story off. At that point in my life I didn't believe in anything that couldn't be proven to exist empirically and this, most assuredly, included ghosts. It was an arrogant creed, but not one uncommon to members of the police service.

When the restaurant manager arrived, he unlocked the door and we went inside. My partner and I searched the building thoroughly, but found nothing physical that might have triggered the burglar alarm. As we left the building, the older cop simply cocked an eyebrow in my direction.

Over the next fifteen years, I responded to other alarm calls at the Hunter and only once were genuine burglars present. Every other time, we found the business secure and, on each occasion I pondered the story of the haunting. True, I still refused to believe in ghosts, but I was forced to acknowledge that the restaurant had more than its fair share of alarms.

By 1997, however, I had come to accept the reality of spectral phenomena. Remembering those late-night calls to the Hunter, I was compelled to conduct an investigation into the purported haunting. I began with some historical research on the location and soon discovered the old cop's information was correct. Up until the 1960s, the grassy bluff now occupied by the Hunter and an adjoining gas station was indeed the site of the Buena Vista Cemetery.

The old graveyard was established in 1884 and some of the

original American residents of Oceanside and Carlsbad were interred there. Estimates on the number of people buried there vary. Some local historians place the number at no more than ten graves, while others assert that as many as forty people were buried in the Buena Vista Cemetery. Furthermore, there is some persuasive evidence that, when the land was prepared for commercial development, all the bodies weren't removed.

How the Hunter came to be constructed on the site of an old cemetery is a sadly familiar tale in the recent history of Southern California. After World War II, the region's population grew explosively and, with it, the highway network. Commercial development adjoining the ubiquitous freeways was also epidemic, for it seemed as if every off-ramp required its own soulless hamburger stand, convenience store, and service station.

By the late 1960s, the eight lanes of Interstate 5 were being extended from Los Angeles to San Diego. When the huge concrete ribbon reached Oceanside, in about 1970, its path came very close to the abandoned graveyard. Not surprisingly, the Buena Vista Cemetery suddenly became a piece of prime real estate. The property was purchased and plans were set to modify the land for business use. But first there was the issue of the bodies.

Local records indicate the corpses from the Buena Vista Cemetery were to be exhumed and re-interred at another regional graveyard. At least that is the "official" account, but there are unanswered questions regarding what actually happened to all the bodies. The formal records on the grisly procedure are disturbingly incomplete and don't really indicate whether all the corpses were removed.

To this day, there are disquieting rumors that the company hired to collect the corpses failed to locate all the graves. This may have happened innocently. The cemetery was abandoned and, over the years, headstones were stolen and graves were consequently rendered unmarked. Some local residents have suggested that there was too little time allotted for the task. They imply that, because there was a rush to prepare the low hill for development, only a cursory search for graves was conducted.

There are other distressing stories that when the construction crews arrived, they found bodies on the site. The workers may have reburied some of the corpses a short distance from their original places of rest. In fact, a laborer from the project admitted that he personally took part in such impromptu burials. The narrative is on a video tape recording in the possession of the Oceanside Historical Society. It's a dismal and chilling story.

The man was employed by a company hired to prepare the hillside for the construction of a freeway junction. But before very long, he realized this was not a typical work site. To begin, there were the piles of discarded headstones. The memorials were haphazardly stacked in area that was to someday become the parking lot of the Hunter Steakhouse. Later, the antique grave markers were broken to bits and added to the fill material beneath an Interstate 5 on-ramp. But other, more ghastly discoveries were to come.

Next came the coffins and bodies. When two or three unidentified graves were located, the authorities were summoned. A local government employee came to the site, said the worker, and unceremoniously tossed the human remains into a burlap sack. From there, the bag was thrown into the trunk of the man's car. The members of the construction crew were distressed by this callous and disrespectful treatment of the dead and resolved to remain silent if any further bodies were found. Instead, the workers would rebury the corpses themselves.

By the worker's estimate, his construction crew located at least three more unidentified bodies. The unclaimed dead were quietly removed from their original graves and moved down the hill toward the placid waters of the lagoon. There, the bodies were carefully reburied together beneath mounds of fill dirt. Although the precise location is not known today, if the bodies aren't actually beneath the Hunter Steakhouse, they are within a stone's throw of the business.

"What we did to the remains was a sincere effort to replace them into a final resting place where no one would mess around with them any further," the worker said of this compassionate act.

Is it any wonder the Hunter Steakhouse is haunted?

Surrounded by lush vegetation, huge gray boulders and tall gnarled pine trees, the restaurant is deceptively large. From the outside, it seems to be a single-story building. Inside, however, the restaurant is revealed to be a three-tiered structure. On the basement level is the bar. The first and second floors are dining areas, configured in such a way that the uppermost level overlooks the floor below.

It is in this spacious area between the first and second floor that an apparition was seen to "walk" in midair. One anonymous witness, whom I will refer to as Denise, was a former employee of the restaurant during the 1980s. She told me of her encounter.

"It was late evening, just after the last customers had gone," she said. "I walked into the dining room and saw this thing moving slowly through the air."

I asked her to describe the "thing."

"It kind of reminded me of a thick mist and it had sort of a human shape. But there weren't any features," Denise replied. "It wasn't like you could see arms, legs, or a head. It was just a human-shaped figure that was floating through the space between the floors. I just stood there and stared at it."

I encouraged Denise to tell me what happened next.

"Well, it just disappeared," said the former waitress. "I was kind of scared, but only because I was surprised. I mean it just isn't normal to walk into a room and see something floating through the air. But I never felt any sense of menace from the thing. The truth be told, I had the feeling it didn't even know I was there."

When asked if she had mentioned the episode to the management or other employees, Denise answered, "I didn't say a word. Even though there had been talk among the staff that the place was haunted, I didn't want people thinking I was nuts. But I know what I saw."

In assessing Denise's account, I was struck by the airborne nature of the apparition. If her story were accurate, the ghost seemed to glide along a surface that no longer exists today. Yet the specter's path may match the original configuration of the bluff before the restaurant was built.

Although aerial phantoms are not a particularly common occurrence, they certainly aren't unheard of. In fact, in many ways these forms of phenomena are similar in function to those instances when a wraith passes through a sealed doorway. Ghosts, it seems, can operate on a separate plane of reality, a place where the topography exists independent of physical modifications wrought by humans.

Denise then described some of the manifestations experienced by other employees. Some claimed to have heard the mutter of disembodied voices, while others complained of being touched by an invisible entity. One worker told Denise that she'd seen an apparition at the base of the stairway in the bar. The ghost was the opaque figure of a woman attired in clothing the witness believed was from the late nineteenth century. The waitress claimed the specter had vanished before her eyes. Based on her own experience, Denise wasn't inclined to dismiss any of the stories.

In closing our conversation, Denise made one thing fundamentally clear: almost everybody who worked at the restaurant accepted the fact that the place was haunted.

In April 1997 I visited the restaurant. Entering the Hunter, I was greeted by a charming hostess, who wasn't greatly surprised when I asked about the haunting. Although she had never personally experienced anything of an unearthly nature, she said it was common knowledge among the employees that the restaurant was haunted. She then referred me to Michael Hall, the manager of the Hunter.

When Mike learned of my interest in the ghosts of the Hunter, he was cheerfully forthcoming. We took seats at a table near a magnificent stone hearth and he began by saying that he was aware the restaurant was built on the former site of the Buena Vista Cemetery. He also made it clear that he remained undecided on the existence of ghosts. Yet he'd seen things happen in the building that he could not rationally explain. Furthermore, over the three and a half years he'd been manager, many employees had reported odd events while working there.

"I began as a bartender here when the restaurant first opened in 1971," said Mike. "Even back then the place had a spooky feeling about it."

Over the passing years, Mike heard a variety of strange stories from other employees. Ghosts were allegedly seen and poltergeist episodes observed. Yet it wasn't until 1995 that the manager had his firsthand encounter with invisible occupants of the restaurant.

"At the time there was a construction crew at the gas station. They were digging up the old gas tanks and the excavation work seemed to really stir things up," he said. At night we began to notice that one or more of the heavy chandeliers over the dining room would periodically take to swaying. Sometimes the movement was as much as three or four inches. We'd never seen that before."

"Could the movement have been caused by earth tremors?" I asked. After all, this was California, where seismic activity is a fact of life.

"I wondered about that too," said Mike. "But it happened so often, I had to accept it wasn't being caused by earthquakes. And those chandeliers didn't take to swinging until after they started to dig up the gas tanks."

"The wind then," I suggested.

"Any wind strong enough to push those chandeliers around would have been felt by the diners and staff," he replied. "Besides, the windows can't be opened. And why would the wind only blow one chandelier at a time, while the others remained motionless?"

The next episode, which was even more difficult to explain, occurred at about the same time the chandeliers had begun their unexplained motion. Mike began the story by directing my attention to three false windows that stood high on the north interior wall and overlooked the first-floor dining room. Behind that façade, said the manager, was a locked attic.

One evening, just after closing, Mike was standing near the reception desk when he was startled by a loud crash from only a few feet away. It was then that he discovered that one of the large and sturdy wooden window frames had somehow disconnected itself from the wall and plummeted to the floor. Fortunately, no one was injured.

"I later examined the frame and saw that the long nails were jutting out of the wood. They weren't damaged or bent," Mike said. "I just don't have a satisfying explanation for how all those nails let loose at once."

Of course, it is possible that the frame's disengagement from the wall was a natural, if uncommon, episode. Oppositely, if the episode was of paranormal origin, it matched precisely the profile of a poltergeist prank: noisy, dramatic, and ultimately harmless.

Mike shared another curious event. "One evening we had a Native American couple down in the bar waiting for a table. A little later, they told the bartender that there was no way they could stay in the restaurant. It was simply too uncomfortable, because of the spirits they sensed. Before leaving, they asked if we were aware the restaurant was built over a burial ground."

Over the years, however, it has been the business' employees who have had the most frequent brushes with the paranormal. As manager, Mike has often reassured upset workers when they described odd events. He offered three other reports received from employees.

A waitress complained of repeatedly having her hair caressed by an invisible hand. These events primarily occurred in a small service alcove in the northwest corner of the first-floor dining room. Eventually, the woman terminated her employment with the restaurant as a consequence of these episodes.

Another female witness, who was described as extremely attractive, told Mike of an auditory encounter. It was late evening, after the restaurant had closed, and the woman was passing through the empty foyer. At that moment, she heard the unmistakable sound of a "wolf whistle." Knowing she was alone, the woman could not account for the noise. (And once more, I noted that some male ghosts continue to be captivated by the fairer sex.)

Next, Mike related the story of a bartender who reported that someone or something was moving the display bottles of wine. Every evening before closing the bar, the worker would meticulously ensure that the wine bottles were neatly arranged on a shelf. Yet when he returned, it wasn't uncommon to find the bottles moved forward, right

THE HUNTER STEAKHOUSE

to the very edge of the platform. Even more curious, none of the bottles ever fell from the shelf.

Searching for a natural explanation, I suggested that perhaps vibrations from the nearby freeway had caused the dislocation. Mike allowed that this was a possibility, but pointed out that while the occurrences were sporadic, the traffic on Interstate 5 certainly wasn't. Moreover, traffic is always appreciably heavier during daytime than late at night, so why, asked Mike, wasn't the phenomena occurring during the day? I didn't have an answer.

With Mike's blessings, I spoke with other Hunter employees. Most knew of the restaurant's haunted reputation and several repeated the story of the female apparition seen near the stairs in the bar. Yet no one could provide the name of the witnessing employee. Several workers, however, were willing to share their personal experiences with me.

Marcos Carrillo started working at the Hunter in 1993 as a dishwasher and, today, busses tables. Although Marcos hadn't seen any ghosts, he'd had several encounters that appeared to corroborate the reports of poltergeist activity.

"When I first began work here, there were times when I had to work until two in the morning to finish the dishes," he said. "It was strange, because when I was all alone in the kitchen, I sometimes heard my name being called. The voice was soft and sounded like a woman."

At first, Marcos assumed it was the male supervisor's voice, somehow distorted by distance. But the assistant manager always denied calling for the worker. Demonstrating sensibility and pluck, Marcos came to accept the episodes as harmless and didn't give them a great deal of attention.

Soon, however, Marcos learned that he wasn't the only employee to hear his or her name being called. Apparently the phenomenon was heard by a number of other workers. Marcos told me of a fellow employee, a young man with strong religious convictions, who unhappily revealed that he too was hearing his name repeatedly called by the invisible woman. Frightened by the disembodied voice, and believing diabolic forces caused it, the man soon quit.

Another interesting fact of late-night maintenance work in the Hunter involved the bathroom doors. "Some nights I would prop the doors open so I could clean and mop the bathrooms," Marcos said. "But many times, I'd see those doors close by themselves, even though I'd used a wedge. It was very weird."

In 1995, Marcos had another eerie encounter. While working late one evening in the second-floor Tapestry Room, he felt a faint rush of air move behind him. It was, asserted Marcos, precisely as if someone had just walked past. Yet there was no one else in the room. There were other curious events. Kitchen lights would be turned off at closing, only to be found on in the morning. Marcos also partially corroborated Mike's observations regarding the chandeliers. Over the past few years he has seen one of the light fixtures sway under its own power. Furthermore, that same chandelier has operated in a peculiar fashion. There were times, said Marcos, when the chandelier's lights would either flicker or turn off of their own accord. Other times, the lights would refuse to work entirely, only to be found operational a short time later.

Above all, asserted Marcos, there was the perpetual sense of being under observation from invisible eyes. Yet he found nothing really frightening about the peculiar atmosphere or poltergeist manifestations. If there were a ghost, it seemed to possess a peaceful temperament.

Marcos shared one final story that seemed to indicate that the wraith could occasionally be helpful. "One busy Saturday night, around 8:30, I was carrying a huge platter full of dirty dishes and glasses. As I moved into the hallway near the service hutch, the tray accidentally hit the wall and began to tilt. Everything started to fall forward and I knew those dishes and glasses were going to all be broken. It would have been very bad. Then, suddenly, I could feel somebody push up against the other side of the tray and it was balanced again. There was nobody there, but somebody stopped that tray from falling."

Another witness was Lance Daniel, a buoyant young man who has worked at the Hunter as a waiter since 1994. Endowed with an interest in paranormal phenomena, Lance was happily willing to share some of his experiences in the restaurant.

"When I first began working at the Hunter, the other employees joked about how every new worker was initiated by the ghosts," Lance chuckled with the memory. "A few nights later, I understood what they meant."

On the evening in question, Lance was in the Tapestry Room taking meal orders from diners, when he felt someone gently nudge his waist. Naturally presuming it was another food server trying to move past, Lance shifted a few feet to the left. He then realized there was nobody standing anywhere near him.

Said Lance: "I guess the customers thought I was acting strangely, but I definitely felt someone press his or her hand against my side."

Not long afterward, he began to experience the same auditory phenomenon reported by Marcos. Lance heard his name being called by an unseen person throughout the restaurant. Most often, however, the voice seemed to originate from the vicinity of the two intersecting stairways, one leading down to the bar and the other leading up to the second floor. Sometimes, said Lance, the voice was that of a woman, but there were occasions when it was a man's tone.

If Lance entertained any doubts that the events were the product of his imagination, they were dispelled when a bus boy also heard the phenomenon. More than a little stunned, the man confirmed that he had just heard a woman's disembodied voice call Lance's name.

Then there was the afternoon when another waiter approached Lance and made a half-panicked request: would he please come to the restroom, because something very odd was happening. Lance complied and, upon entering the washroom, instantly understood why the other employee was so anxious. Emanating from the ceiling was the sound of arrhythmic pounding.

"It was loud and went on for about five minutes," Lance said. "At first we hoped the noise might have been caused by someone moving tables on the second floor, but the sounds seemed to be right above us. This was a problem, because there is nothing above the bathrooms but the attic and you need a key to get in there. In the end, neither of us could explain the sounds."

Like Marcos, Lance had also noted the electric lights operated strangely in the restaurant. The place seemed prone to power surges and the lights were constantly flickering. He was also present when the window frame crashed to the floor. Finally, he had repeatedly experienced the unmistakable feeling of being watched by an unseen presence.

"Still, I've never been frightened," said Lance, flashing a smile. "I have the sense the ghosts are a benevolent presence and are just interested in what we're doing."

After these initial interviews, I returned to the Hunter a few nights later so that I might interview the night crew. I found Rick "Spike" Spikerman tending bar and asked him about the haunting.

"Well, I can't say for a fact that I've *seen* a ghost here. Don't even know if I believe in them," declared Spike. "But I've had a few things happen that I don't have an explanation for."

Spike then told me of a peculiar observation he once made while in the men's restroom. While washing his hands at the sink,

Spike looked in the mirror and saw a nebulous and misty shape flowing along the wall behind him. The bartender turned quickly to get a better look at the form, but it disappeared.

"Now I was the only person in the room," Spike explained, "but I know what I saw."

Another episode occurred after closing time. Spike and several other employees were relaxing in the bar when, without warning, the ceiling lights swiftly dimmed and then resumed their original brightness. One of the workers nervously suggested the building had just been subjected to a power surge. But Spike knew this wasn't the case, because the television and ancillary lights were unaffected by the "surge." Rather, it seemed as if someone were playing with the light controls.

Spike went to the storeroom, where the dimmer switch was located, expecting to find a human intruder. Yet the small room was empty. When the bartender reached for the rheostat dial, he felt all the hairs on his hand and lower arm stand straight up. It was almost as if he'd moved his hand into some kind of electrical field. At the same time, it was unlikely that a defective switch caused the sensation, for Spike's hand hadn't yet made physical contact with the rheostat.

"I've adjusted that light switch for years, but never before or since have I ever felt that kind of electric charge," Spike quietly stated.

The bartender also confirmed some of the information provided by Mike Hall regarding the occasional baffling movement of wine bottles. "One night I watched a bottle of Corona Beer just fall from the shelf," Spike said. "Later, a couple of us tried to shake and vibrate the shelf to see if we could make it happen again. We even balanced a couple beer bottles right on the edge, but we couldn't get them to budge."

Consistent with the other witnesses, Spike too has heard his name softly called by an unseen person. Ordinarily, this occurred after closing, when he was alone and cleaning the bar. And, as with the other employees, Spike didn't attach too much significance to the episodes. The events were harmless and hardly worthy of notice.

However, Spike did pass on an old and somewhat frightening story from the restaurant that involved a former bartender. One evening while the man was working in the storeroom, he watched as a large dispenser box of Chablis wine suddenly pitched forward from a shelf and crashed to the floor, narrowly missing the bartender. This was remarkable, explained Spike, for such boxes can weigh as much as twenty pounds and aren't known to move under their own power.

With this story and the accounts of wine and beer bottles being upended, I wondered if one of the Hunter's wraiths bore an antipathy for alcoholic beverages. This suspicion was further strengthened when I spoke with my next witness, Jeff Gardner, who works as a waiter, bartender, and night manager. Indeed, Jeff had experienced an odd event involving alcoholic beverages only a few days before our interview.

"I was tending bar and opened the small refrigerator to get a bottle of wine," he said. "Thirty seconds later, I went back to open the refrigerator again and found it locked. Now there was nobody else behind the bar and the manager is the only person with the key to the fridge. Yet someone locked it."

Jeff went on to describe some other uncanny incidents.

One evening, after closing time, Jeff was preparing to lock up and depart when his attention was drawn to the credit card terminal. The device had begun to operate and Jeff watched in amazement as the device expelled a long slip of blank receipt paper. It seemed to the night manager as if someone was experimenting with the machine.

"The only way for the paper to be advanced like that is to physically press a button on the keypad," explained Jeff. "But I was the only person in the restaurant and never touched the buttons."

Another night, while working in the second-floor Wine Room, Jeff observed a wall-mounted light behaving strangely. The brass fixture and glass light sheath began to rock back and forth quickly, moving as much as an inch. Searching for a rational explanation, Jeff wondered if the phenomenon was created by an earthquake, or perhaps from vibrations caused by artillery fire from nearby Camp Pendleton. Yet none of the lights were similarly affected.

Jeff too has heard his name called by an unseen man, often when he is the only person in the building. Moreover, like the other employees, he often feels his actions are monitored by an invisible presence.

My next witness was Stephanie Daniel, a food server who had her own unearthly encounter in the Wine Room. The young woman described that event as we stood in the foyer near the hostess's desk.

Almost a year earlier, just after closing time, she caught a momentary glimpse of an older man standing near an east-facing window. The man was attired in antique apparel and appeared fully physical. Stephanie stopped to peer at the curious figure and noticed that the man seemed to be staring through the window at the distant hills. A moment later, the wraith vanished. She subsequently learned that a former waitress had also observed the male ghost in precisely the same location.

On another occasion, Stephanie and another employee were in the lady's restroom when they were startled by the sound of loud knocking emanating from the ceiling. Darting outside, Stephanie checked the adjoining door to the liquor storage room, which is also the only access route to the attic. That door was padlocked from the outside.

"There was nobody in the attic, so there's no way somebody was up there, playing a practical joke," she said. "In my opinion, our ghosts stay up in the attic when the restaurant is busy. It's quiet and isolated up there."

While Stephanie and I spoke, a peculiar thing happened. Suddenly the air became cool and slightly moist. Stephanie stared at me and whispered, "Do you feel that?"

I did and told her so. The chill was not caused by the wind, nor was the air conditioner on. Yet the temperature had dropped about ten degrees in a matter of a few seconds. What's more, only a few steps away, the atmosphere felt completely normal. It was a classic cold spot and it seemed as one of the ghosts had decided to eavesdrop on our conversation. Finally, I told the invisible entity to go away and stop being an annoyance. After about thirty seconds, the cold spot dissipated.

"That happens all the time here," said a slightly shaken Stephanie. "I guess someday I'll get used to it."

Another witness who saw an apparition in the restaurant was

THE HUNTER STEAKHOUSE

Jason Prichard, who has worked as a waiter at the Hunter since 1992. Jason said he had heard the stories of a haunting, but wasn't prepared to believe the accounts, for the prospect of a ghost in the eatery was just too incredible to accept. He remained a skeptic until 1995, when he saw the ghost.

"It was about 11:30 and I was down in the bar talking with the manager. We were the only ones in the building," said Jason. "But as I walked up the stairs, I saw a man move across the dining room."

The dining room was dark, but Jason was absolutely certain he'd seen a male form stroll toward the service alcove. Concerned there was an intruder in the restaurant, the waiter went to investigate, but found both the room and alcove empty. Perhaps significantly, it was in the same small service room where several other employees had had unearthly encounters.

"I'll admit, I was a little anxious when I couldn't find anybody there," he concluded. "But if it was the ghost, I guess it wasn't that big a deal."

In summary, the restaurant is home to apparitions, poltergeist activity, and disembodied voices, but one thing is clear: the entities don't appear malicious, merely playful.

Since several of the reports of phenomena seemed connected with the attic, I was determined to explore the room. Equipped with a flashlight, I climbed through the crawl hole and began an inspection of the premises. The room was dark and boxes lay stacked haphazardly on the floor. Overhead, the rafters were decorated with cobwebs. I remained in the attic for about twenty minutes, but saw and heard nothing.

As might be expected, the groundwater connection to haunting remained consistent at the Hunter. Immediately to the south of the restaurant are the Buena Vista Creek and Lagoon, the latter being quite sizeable. There seems water enough to assist in the generation of ghost phenomena.

So, if you are ever in the mood for a meal, enlivened by the potential of an encounter with a spook, you cannot do better than the Hunter Steakhouse in Oceanside. After all, it is a place renowned for its steaks, seafood, and *spirits.*

*　　　　　*　　　　　*

Immediately to the east of The Hunter is a now-abandoned gas station. Since it too was built atop the Buena Vista Cemetery, I wondered if the paranormal activity extended to the vacant building. In April 1997, at about 10:30 p.m., I decided to find out. Equipped with a heavy flashlight, camera, my briar pipe, and tobacco pouch, I embarked on a ghost expedition.

The night was pleasant, with a slight breeze blowing off the ocean. A dozen yards to the east, traffic roared along Interstate 5. Although a chain-link fence surrounded the gas station, I was able to locate a gap in the barrier. I cautiously approached the ramshackle structure, for there was an excellent chance I might discover transients within.

Yet when I made my way through a ragged hole in one of the service bay doors, I was somewhat surprised to find the interior empty. I shined my flashlight throughout the building and saw that the floor was covered with broken glass, bald tires, and old Texaco posters. It looked as if the former occupants had vacated the place with undue speed. But what struck me as most curious was the lack of transients. Oceanside has a fairly large number of homeless and they commonly seek quarters in abandoned structures. Yet there was no evidence that anyone had been in temporary residence. There were no signs of campfires, no discarded toilet tissue, and no drug paraphernalia. Why, I wondered, had the transients ignored this available shelter?

The answer came soon enough. As I stepped from the garage into the office, I was suddenly enveloped by a curtain of cool, moist air. Chills swept up my arms, to my back, and then up and down my spine. Never in my life had I experienced such a powerful sensation of ethereal cold. Even more disturbing was the realization that I was not at all welcome in the gas station. Clearly, I was an intruder.

I spoke aloud to the entity, advising I meant no harm and then retreated a few feet. Sitting down on a pile of tires, I lit my pipe and asked the ghost to show itself. For the next two hours I sat in the gloom, all the while aware that I was being watched by an invisible and unhappy person. Yet he never showed himself. Occasionally I heard a faint scratching sound in the rafters and was strangely comforted by the knowledge the noise was caused by rats.

When I finally left the gas station, I understood why the homeless avoided the building.

*   *   *

An interesting collateral aspect to the haunting of the Hunter is that it appears to be part of a larger ghost reservation extending along a road known as Vista Way. Over the years, at least three other structures along the south side of Vista Way have been the sites of ghost and poltergeist phenomena.

Rosa Avila lived in one such house on the 900 block of Vista Way from 1972 through 1977. The location was only three blocks west of the Hunter Steakhouse. The owner of a gift shop in the Oceanside Harbor area, Rosa is an older woman with lovely brown eyes and a warm smile. She is also strongly intuitive and quite spiritually inclined. Yet it took no great psychic powers to sense there wasn't something quite right about her new home.

"From the beginning we could hear the sound of loud footsteps on the roof over the kid's bedroom," recalled Rosa. "The first few times we ran outside to see if there was someone on the roof. But there was never anyone there."

The auditory phenomenon occurred night and day. Sometimes, as Rosa's children were getting ready for school in the morning, they'd report hearing "the man on the roof." Determined to learn the origin of the noises, Rosa conducted some research and discovered that the former owner had died in the room now occupied by her children. Clearly, the sounds were connected to his death. But instead of giving way to panic over the presence of a ghost, Rosa did something useful.

"When we first moved in, I found the man's Bible. So I got it out and sat down in the bedroom. For hours, I prayed and read Scripture aloud. Then I would tell the spirit he was dead and could leave."

The merciful application of prayer was apparently successful, for the footfalls never recurred. Yet there were some other eerie episodes. Rosa heard spectral music in the house several times. At first, she presumed her teenaged-children had left the stereo on. However, one day she decided to search out the origin of the music. As each room was checked, Rosa confirmed that all the stereo equipment was turned off. It was then that she realized the music seemed to be emanating from the ground.

"It was the most melodious and lovely tune I've ever heard," she said. "But it was coming up from the floor and that was…disturbing, because we didn't have a basement."

Murmuring a prayer, Rosa left the room. No matter how splendid the music, the unearthly source of the sound was simply too unsettling. Eventually, the music stopped.

A few months later, Rosa learned that her neighbors were also enduring a series of apparition and poltergeist episodes. A young couple who lived two houses to the west often reported seeing a tenuous, human-shaped form emerge from the master bedroom and glide down the hall. Even more troubling were the late-night pranks by an invisible joker. Night after night, the couple was jolted awake as the bedclothes were yanked from the bed. Discovering that Rosa had been successful in evicting her noisy specter, they asked her to investigate.

"I walked into the house and looked around. Then I came to the master bedroom and opened the closet. There was a musty, decaying smell. I reminded me of death." Her nose wrinkled with the memory.

She felt that the closet was the locus of the haunting and suggested the couple embark on a regimen of prayer. However, she subsequently learned that the young woman had begun making efforts to communicate with the entity by means of an Ouija board; not for the purpose of evicting the ghost but for entertainment. Believing that nothing good could come from such reckless dabbling, Rosa refused to have anything further to do with the couple.

One final note: when Rosa learned that the Buena Vista Cemetery once stood only a few blocks to the east of her old home, she was not surprised. In fact, she thought it might well explain the plethora of paranormal activity along Vista Way.

*   *   *

Another few blocks directly west is yet another haunted building, although it would be more accurate to describe the phenomena as poltergeist activity. Oddly enough, I learned of the events while working as a police sergeant.

It was the summer of 1995 and I was in the Watch Commander's office when the telephone rang. On the line was a middle-aged woman who demanded to know if a suicide or murder had ever occurred in her Vista Way home. When I asked why she wanted this information, she reluctantly began to relate a series of odd events occurring in her house. Both she and another female roommate had heard unaccountable raps on the walls and repeatedly found locked doors and windows open. Moreover, they would frequently discover personal items missing, only to find them in plain sight a few days later. And always there was the sense of an unseen person in the house.

I asked the lady if she thought her house were haunted. Immediately, she burst into tears and agreed, but said that she was an idiot for having called the police about a ghost. I calmed the woman and told her I would come to the home as soon as possible. In the meantime, I dispatched an officer to the residence in an effort to restore emotional equilibrium.

When I explained the errand to the officer, I could tell that he was uncomfortable with the assignment. Nonetheless, he went to the house to assist the women. I left the police station about fifteen minutes later and, as I drove up to the residence, I found the officer and the two women standing in the front yard, peering anxiously at the house. As I approached the nervous trio, the cop muttered, "Jesus, sarge, I'm glad you're here."

Obviously something had happened, so I asked him to tell me more. His story was funny, in a macabre way. After arriving at the house, the officer had listened to the stories of spectral activity with an impassive face, yet he later admitted he was becoming increasingly disturbed. When the women finished their account, the officer asked, "What are you trying to say, lady? Is this house haunted?"

At that moment, a loud crashing sound erupted from the ceiling above the officer. The noise, he asserted, was like a piano being dropped on the rafters. Both women began to scream and one fainted. Once the officer revived the fainting victim, all three left the house post haste. Then the officer produced a tiny audiocassette recorder and told me the tape had been running during the encounter. He turned the device on and I listened. The event occurred precisely as described and the banging sound was clearly audible.

Both the officer and I later entered the house and checked the interior, but could find nothing to have caused the sound. We calmed the frightened women and told them that, as much as we wanted to help, unruly poltergeist behavior was beyond the purview of the city police.

I subsequently learned that the women had moved to new lodgings. Several months later, however, I was sent to the house in response to a "disturbing the peace" call. Upon arrival, I found a raucous party in progress at the residence. I knocked on the door and spoke with the new occupants. They were two men in their early 20s, who quickly agreed to turn down the music and keep the drunks inside the house.

Then, I asked one of the residents what it was like to live in a haunted house. The man's jaw dropped and he demanded to know how I was aware the house was haunted. As we conversed, I learned that the poltergeist phenomena had continued. Doors were opening, raps were heard, personal items were hidden, and there was the omnipresent sense of being watched by an invisible entity. Yet the man and his roommate weren't inordinately disturbed.

"Like, it's just a ghost, man," drawled the young fellow. "Hell, I've had worse roommates; lots worse."

*   *   *

Is it merely coincidence that there are at least four haunted buildings near the desecrated site of the Buena Vista Cemetery? Until more is known about the intangible phenomena of ghosts and poltergeists, the best we can do is only guess at the connection. In the meantime, research will continue and I will do my best to contribute to the reservoir of knowledge. I can't imagine a greater adventure.

THE SPECTRAL STOWAWAY: THE HAUNTING OF STAR OF INDIA

With its superb harbor, San Diego is a city rich in maritime tradition. The first European settlers arrived by ship and the survival of the fledgling colony was utterly dependent on supplies that were delivered by sea. In later years, the harbor was an increasingly busy place as merchantmen visited the port to trade European and American luxuries for stacks of cowhides. It was a ship, in the form of the USS frigate *Cyane* that wrought the most enduring change, raising the conquering American flag over San Diego in 1846.

There have also been tragedies on the bay. Yankee Jim Robinson began his journey toward the hangman's rope while riding the harbor waters. The most lethal episode occurred in July 1905 when the boilers of the USS *Bennington* blew up with a thunderous roar, killing 62 men and injuring dozens more. And where there's been a calamity, you will often find ghosts. Therefore, it should come as no surprise that a haunted ship is moored on the San Diego waterfront.

Her name is *Star of India* and the black-hulled ship is one of three vintage craft comprising the San Diego Maritime Museum. *Star of India* is not her original name. Originally christened *Euterpe*, the three-mast ship was launched from Great Britain's Isle of Man in 1863 and for 35 years sailed under a British flag. *Euterpe* was a curious mixture of old and new features. She sported a then modern iron hull, but was not equipped with steam engines, relying entirely on sails and wind to journey around the world.

Euterpe carried Indian jute to England, European emigrants to Australia and New Zealand, and Hawaiian sugar to San Francisco. She also seems to have had more than her share of troubles. There were damaging collisions with other ships, a peaceful mutiny of her crew, and a number of deaths of passengers and crew. Then in 1898 the ship was sold to an American firm and her glory days were apparently finished. Renamed *Star of India*, she was converted into a bark, and set to work at salmon fishing in Alaska.

In 1923, *Star of India* was retired and unceremoniously left to decay in an Oakland estuary. The hull began to rust and grass grew on the deck, a sad ending for a ship that had survived savage Pacific typhoons, hull-ravaging reefs, icebergs, and the stormy rigors of the Cape Horn passage. Then, in 1927, a group of San Diego maritime aficionados purchased the hulk for $9000 and towed it to San Diego. The plan was to renovate the ship and convert it into a floating museum, but with the onset of the Great Depression there was little money for such an endeavor. Nearly a half-century would pass before the restoration work was completed.

During the intervening years *Star of India* was used as a bayside set for a staging of *The Pirates of Penzance*, was apparently briefly employed as a floating brothel by an unscrupulous caretaker, and there was periodic talk of towing the old ship out and sinking her. During World War II, the US Navy declared the ship's masts to be a hazard to aviation and had them crudely trimmed.

After the war there was a slow but concerted campaign to restore *Star of India*. Donations were collected and a small cadre of dedicated volunteers labored to bring the grand old ship back to life. They were successful and in 1976, *The Star of India* unfurled her sails and took to the sea once more. Indeed, she is today the oldest active sailing ship in the world. You can tour the ship throughout the year, but for the ghost aficionado the best time to visit is at Halloween when the museum offers chilling ghostly tours. With its *Flying Dutchman* décor of shredded sails and unearthly black lights, the old bark is particularly alluring. Better yet, there is apparently a real ghost in residence.

In June 1999, I decided it was time to investigate the haunting.

Located on the waterfront near the downtown district, the San Diego Maritime Museum's trio of antique vessels is a charming and anachronistic incongruity in a harbor that is home to giant aircraft carriers, modern yachts, and bulky container ships. On the day of my visit, the decks and rigging of *Star of India* were busy with activity. Employees and volunteers were varnishing woodwork, scrubbing decks, and painting the upper portion of the mast in preparation for a short voyage in July.

I moved about the ship, making my inquiries. Some of the employees were genially dismissive of the ghost reports, while others refused to categorically deny the stories of haunting. After all, the sea has a way of endowing a sliver of mysticism to even the most pragmatic mariner. Later, I asked Joseph Ditler, the Director of Development for the San Diego Maritime Museum, if the iron-hulled bark was a ghost preserve.

"All ships are haunted, but some more than others," said Ditler, who has been with the museum for over a decade. "*Star of India* has a very special atmosphere. I'm not prone to flights of imagination, but if you stand on the decks, you can't help but sense the spirits of the seamen and passengers who sailed on her."

Although no apparitions have been seen recently, Ditler told me that during the 1920s an onboard caretaker reported several encounters with the ghost of a teenaged boy. Furthermore, there have been repeated accounts of nighttime visitors being touched by a disembodied hand. These episodes appear to have occurred most frequently near the mainmast and Ditler thought it was likely the apparition sightings and gentle poltergeist activity were evidence of the spirit of John Campbell, a stowaway who died aboard the ship in 1884. The story is sad, but all too typical of the hard life of a nineteenth-century sailor.

In May 1884, *Star of India* (still known as *Euterpe*) departed Glasgow en route for New Zealand. A few days out, three young stowaways were discovered and put to work. One was a teenaged orphan named John Campbell, who had chosen to escape his unhappy life of grinding poverty for the adventure of the sea. But on June 26, 1884, the young Scot discovered that adventure does not come without risk. Campbell was working near the top of the mainmast when he incautiously waved at a friend. Losing his grip, Campbell plunged over 100 feet to the wooden deck, horribly mangling his legs. The unfortunate youth lingered three days, mercifully unconscious, before dying and he was buried at sea.

Considering the tragic circumstances of Campbell's demise, I wondered why his spirit chose to remain on the ship. Ditler offered a perceptive potential answer: "John Campbell was willing to risk anything rather than remain in Glasgow. By stowing away, he created a completely new life – a life where he had some control over his future – and because of that, those few weeks on *Star of India* were probably the happiest Campbell ever knew."

It was an intriguing notion. Perhaps some ghosts chose to remain in a place because it imparts joyful memories.

There is another locale on the ship that routinely provokes shivers from visitors and that is the chain locker in the ship's forecastle. Ditler told me it is a common occurrence for museum guests to report an eerie cold spot or ask staffers if someone died in the claustrophobic enclosure. And someone apparently did. Tradition holds that during one of *Star of India's* expeditions to the salmon grounds of Alaska in the early 1900s, a Chinese crewmember was trapped in the chain locker as the anchor was being weighed. He died, crushed beneath the heavy chains.

But there may be another ghost in the San Diego Maritime Museum and it resides on the adjoining steam-powered ferryboat *Berkeley*, which houses a splendid gallery of nautical displays. The *Berkeley* is a historic ship in her own right and was a San Francisco fixture from 1898 to 1958 as she carried passengers back and forth across the bay. But the *Berkeley's* moment of glory was in the days after the Great Earthquake of 1906 when she operated 24 hours a day to carry victims of the temblor and fire across the bay to safety. The Maritime Museum obtained the vessel in 1973 and today the *Berkeley* is considered by many to be the best preserved nineteenth-century ferryboat in existence.

STAR OF INDIA

Is it possible that one of her bygone passengers is still aboard?

Chuck Thomas is a painter and has worked for the Maritime Museum since 1975. At the outset of our talk he made it thoroughly clear that he wasn't interested in ghosts, nor was he in the habit of looking for them, much less seeing them. Yet Chuck was at a loss to explain an episode that occurred in the late 1970s.

"Early one morning, I was working on the *Berkeley's* main deck. It was real foggy – classic pea soup fog – and you could smell just how old the ship was. It's the smell of old paint, varnish, and the sea," said Chuck. "Anyway, I was on the port side, just about amidships, when I noticed someone walking along the deck, through the fog. This was very strange because there was no sound and I knew I was the only one on board."

Chuck peered at the diffuse figure and was just able to make out the image of a gentleman wearing a fedora-style hat. Then the shape vanished into the dense mist. Startled by the sighting, Chuck rushed to the spot where he'd last observed the man, but could see no one.

"I've never seen anything since," Chuck said with a laugh. "And it wouldn't bother me if things stay that way."

I conducted some research in the hope of identifying the ghost and learned there had been several deaths aboard *Berkeley*, the most dramatic occurring on Friday, January 13, 1911. The *Berkeley* was churning its way across San Francisco Bay when a large explosion gutted the men's restroom on the main deck. One man, John O. Norbom, was killed and another five passengers were injured. Once the boat was docked, police investigated the disaster and the story made headlines in newspapers throughout the region. The detectives eventually came to the conclusion that Norbom had been carrying a bottle of nitroglycerine in his pocket and he'd somehow dropped the explosive.

But is the ghost the fumble-fingered spirit of John Norbom? Well, however dramatic the circumstances of his death, this is unlikely because the ghost Chuck Thomas saw was wearing a fedora. That style of hat was not popular in 1911 and seems to indicate a phantom from a later decade. Therefore, it seems more probable the figure was merely a psychic imprint from one of the thousands of long-departed passengers of the ferryboat.

It's also possible that the *Berkeley's* specter and John Campbell's ghost on *Star of India* are proof of a phantasmagoric law of the sea: nautical ghosts never take shore leave.

(The San Diego Maritime Museum is located at 1306 North Harbor Drive, San Diego, CA 92101. Telephone: (619) 234-9153. The museum is open daily from 9 a.m. to 8 p.m. There is an admission fee of $5 for adults; $4 for juniors (ages 13-17); $2 for children (ages 6-12); under age 6, seniors, and active-duty military are free. Contact the museum for information on the Halloween tours. For additional information, you can also visit their website at www.sdmaritime.com.)

EPILOGUE: A BRIEF PRIMER ON GHOST ENCOUNTERS

On our nightly tours past the haunted places of Old Town San Diego, guests often used to ask the same questions regarding ghost and poltergeist phenomena. Lurid films and melodramatic books, appearing under the guise of "true" ghost stories, have created an enormous number of misconceptions about spectral encounters. Therefore, I thought it might be instructive to conclude this book by offering a few tips on how to interact with a spook.

How can I go about seeing a ghost?

Curiously enough, one of the best ways to make sure you *won't* have an encounter with a specter is to set out in search of one. To illustrate, I've visited dozens of haunted buildings for the specific purpose of locating ghosts, but have never seen an apparition under those conditions. Perhaps my "performance anxiety" rendered the atmosphere unsuitable for a ghost sighting. Oppositely, on the two occasions I saw apparitions, I was relaxed and my thoughts unfocused.

We might then conclude that the human witness must be at ease to experience ghost phenomena. This passive mental state could be considered analogous to a motor vehicle with the clutch engaged. However, when we see an apparition, we spontaneously "pop the clutch," thereby terminating the condition that allowed us to perceive the ghost.

Another complicating factor is that spectral phenomena occur on an irregular basis. Ordinarily, haunted sites are only periodically active with interludes of calm that can extend for months. My guests often complained that they visited the Whaley House or other famous haunted place and saw nothing. But this is to be expected, for specters operate on an unfathomable schedule.

What do ghosts look like?

Specters can appear in a variety of forms. Indeed, multiple witnesses to a ghost might view the apparition with different levels of clarity. Some ghosts can appear fully corporeal and initially be mistaken for a living person. Other apparitions manifest as translucent forms or vaporous mists with a vague human shape. Another variation is the partial-figure apparition, where the upper portion of the phantasm is usually visible.

Why the disparity in form and clarity? As mentioned previously, the human observer plays a fundamental role in deciphering the ghostly image. Recall the analogy of the television receiver offered in the preface. In a group of observers, some will be precisely "tuned" to the spectral broadcast frequency and view the specter distinctly, while others receive a weaker signal and see it less clearly.

What should I do if I see a ghost?

Rule Number One is not to be frightened. Certainly their spontaneous appearance can be startling, but ghosts cannot hurt you. Indeed, you run a far greater risk of injuring yourself by a panicked response than from anything a revenant spirit might do. Relax and take the opportunity to fully participate in one of the most ancient elements of the human experience: an encounter with a ghost. Afterward, you might want to try and sketch what you observed and make some notes on the experience.

You said ghosts can't hurt you, so how does that explain "The Amityville Horror"?

Although *The Amityville Horror* was widely touted as a "true story," there is not a shred of quality evidence that anything ghostly ever happened at the notorious Long Island home. Indeed, there are compelling circumstantial facts that *The Amityville Horror* was a very lucrative hoax. When reading this class of "true" ghost books, it is useful to keep one dictum in mind: the more sensational the story, the less likely it is to be true.

Do visible apparitions ever speak?

The answer is seldom. At most haunted places the phenomena will either be audible or visible, but rarely both at the same time. Specters have been observed moving their lips, but there is no accompanying sound. Conversely, spectral voices have been heard without the appearance of a visible ghost. It's almost as if the phantasm possesses only enough energy to manifest in a single mode.

The only routine exception to this rule occurs during a "crisis apparition," which cannot be properly considered a ghostly episode. "Crisis apparitions" are those instances when a family member, loved one, or close friend makes an appearance either shortly before or after that person's death. In such encounters, the specter often passes on a farewell message to the stunned beholder. Unlike standard ghost phenomena, the "crisis apparition" is generally a one-time event and the spirit frequently demonstrates a specific purpose for the visit.

Do poltergeists behave anything like what I've seen in films?

I often told my guests that the first portion of the Steven Spielberg film *Poltergeist* was a reasonably accurate portrayal of such a spectral infestation. However, the second half of the movie was deliciously terrifying and pure bunkum. Most poltergeist phenomena involve the gentle manipulation of physical environment; lights are turned on and off, electrical appliances operate without human control, personal items are hidden and then returned, and audible raps are heard. Sometimes, the poltergeist is attracted to the bathroom, where faucets are turned on and toilets are flushed. It's spooky, but not particularly menacing.

It must be admitted that occasionally poltergeist phenomena can be quite destructive, but such instances are in the extreme minority. To put this into perspective, you probably stand a far better chance of winning the jackpot of your state lottery twice in a row than of encountering this sort of violent haunting.

Are you a "ghostbuster"?

No. My research work at haunted sites is basically passive in nature. I collect witness statements, make some limited use of electronic equipment, and conduct historical research on the site. Furthermore, I'm not sanguine regarding many of the grandiose claims of the more commercially oriented and flamboyant psychics who assert that they can unfailingly rid a place of spectral infestation. And I want to offer a gentle warning: be very cautious of the psychic who demands a fee to evict ghosts. Sometimes these "helpful" folks want a pretty fair chunk of money and there is absolutely no guarantee they can eliminate a wraith.

What is your opinion of the Ouija board?

I believe the Ouija board can produce intelligible messages, but that does not necessarily mean that it is an infallible e-mail system between this world and that of the spirits. True, some communication appears to originate from discarnate sources, but the messages can also be caused by involuntary muscle movements and surreptitious manipulation by practical jokers in a séance group. Furthermore, I'm not enormously impressed with the quality of communication. Occasionally, a bit of accurate information can be derived from the board, but all too often the messages are nonsensical or deliberately false.

Some stern religionists claim that the Ouija board is an instrument of the Devil, but I believe the planchette message system is no more intrinsically wicked than a hammer, saw, or other tool. It all depends on how the implement is used. The greatest hazard is that the user might develop an unhealthy obsession for such communication. It's for this reason that, although it is advertised as a harmless toy, I would never allow children to play with the Ouija board.

How can I become a ghost researcher?

It's remarkably easy. You might begin by checking your telephone book for a local paranormal or ghost investigation group. Such organizations are usually happy to embrace new members. Another venue is to join the Ghost Research Society (P.O. Box 205, Oak Lawn, IL 60454-0205). A national network of investigators, the Ghost

Research Society can provide you a list of regional contacts and information on the best methods to examine spectral phenomena.

You might also want to acquaint yourself with the more sensible literature on ghosts. Works by several authors, including Richard Senate, Arthur Myers, Antoinette May, and Colin Wilson, are available at most major bookstores. Another "must" for your ghost library is Dennis William Hauck's book, *Haunted Places: The National Directory*, which is probably the most comprehensive listing of spectral sites in the United States.

One final piece of advice: when you are finally prepared to investigate your first haunted house, don't expect to encounter paranormal phenomena. Ghosts don't perform on demand. But if something uncanny does occur, keep your head and do your best to observe the event dispassionately. Afterward, make comprehensive notes and write a report on the experience.

Haunted places dot the American landscape. Isn't it about time you paid one a visit?

Author John J. Lamb

Although John Lamb was born in Michigan, the bulk of his childhood and adolescence was spent in southern California. A graduate of John H. Francis Polytechnic High School (Sun Valley, California), Lamb always excelled in writing and history.

His interest in ghosts began in 1995 when he saw an apparition of a young Confederate soldier, in broad daylight, in a gift shop in Gettysburg, Pennsylvania. Since that time, Lamb combined his love for history and interest in paranormal phenomena to begin a career in writing that resulted in *San Diego Specters*. The author is the Southern California Regional Coordinator for the nationwide Ghost Research Society and is a regular contributor to the GRS journal *Ghost Trackers*.

BIBLIOGRAPHY

Cleland, Robert Glass. *The Cattle on a Thousand Hills: Southern California, 1850 –1890.* San Marino, CA: The Henry Huntington Library and Art Gallery, 1969.

Crawford, Richard W. *Stranger Than Fiction: Vignettes of San Diego History.* San Diego, CA: San Diego Historical Society, 1995.

Eysenck, Hans J. and Sargent, Carl. *Explaining the Unexplained: Mysteries of the Paranormal.* Avery Publishing, 1993.

Fodor, Nandor. *Between Two Worlds.* West Nyack, NY: Parker Publishing Company, 1964.

Fuller, Theodore W. *San Diego Originals: Profiles of the movers and shakers of California's first community.* Pleasant Hill, CA: California Profiles Publications, 1987.

Guiley, Rosemary Ellen. *Harper's Encyclopedia of Mystical and Paranormal Experience.* San Francisco, CA: Harper Collins Publishers, 1991.

———. *The Encyclopedia of Ghosts and Spirits.* New York: Facts on File, Inc., 1992.

———. *Atlas of the Mysterious in North America.* New York: Facts on File, Inc., 1995.

Handbook of Parapsychology. New York: Van Nostrand Reinhold Company, 1977.

Hauck, Dennis William. *Haunted Places: The National Directory: a guidebook to Ghostly abodes, sacred sites, UFO landings, and other supernatural locations.* New York: Penguin Books, 1996.

Holzer, Hans. *Ghosts of the Golden West.* New York: The Bobbs-Merril Co, Inc., 1972.

——. *The Handbook of Parapsychology.* New York: Manor Books, 1975.

Lockwood, Herbert. *Fallout From the Skeleton's Closet.* San Diego, CA: The San Diego Independent, 1968.

——. *Skeleton's Closet Revisited.* Spring Valley, CA: Bailey & Associates.

MacMullen, Jerry. *Star of India: The Log of an Iron Ship.* San Diego, CA: Maritime Museum Association of San Diego, 1961, 1993.

May, Antoinette. *Haunted Houses of California: A Ghostly Guide to Haunted Houses And Wandering Spirits.* San Carlos, CA: Wide World Publishing/Tetra, 1993.

Myers, Arthur. *The Ghostly Gazetteer: America's most fascinating haunted landmarks.* Chicago, IL: Contemporary Books, 1990.

Reading, June. *The Thomas Whaley House.* San Diego, CA: Historical Shrine Foundation of San Diego County, 1960.

Senate, Richard. *The Haunted Southland: Ghosts of Southern California.* Ventura, CA: Charon Press, 1994.

——. *The Ghost Stalkers Guide to Haunted California.* Ventura, CA: Charon Press, 1998.

Schwartz, Henry. *Tales of Old Town.* San Diego, CA: San Miguel Press, 1980.

Tyrrell, G.N.M. *Apparitions.* New York: Collier Books, 1963.

White, Gail. *Haunted San Diego: A Historic Guide to San Diego's Favorite Haunts.* San Diego, CA: Tecolote Publications, 1995.

Wilson, Colin. *Poltergeist: A Study in Destructive Haunting.* St. Paul, MN: Llewellyn Worldwide, Ltd., 1983.

——. *Beyond the Occult.* New York: Carroll & Graf Publishers, 1991.

Wlodarski, Robert and Anne. *The Haunted Whaley House: A History and Guide to the Most Haunted House in America.* West Hills, CA: G-HOST Publishing, 1997.

WPA Guide to California, The. New York: Pantheon Books, 1984.

INDEX

Breinigsville, PA USA
05 May 2010
237382BV00001B/2/A